"Andrea proposes a multilingual equity agenda focusing on students who have historically been marginalized in school, especially those whose language practices have been racialized or otherwise stigmatized as a result of deficit ideologies, institutional racism, and deskilling approaches to teaching. She brilliantly illustrates the intersectionality of language, inequality, and social justice as she explores the past, present, and future of these issues."

—**Margarita Calderón, PhD,** Professor Emerita,
Johns Hopkins University

"For any practitioner, leader, or advocate committed to equity, *Multilingual Justice in Schools* is an indispensable guide to building schools that belong to all. It provides us with tools to recognize, redress, and cultivate environments where multilingual learners' full linguistic repertoires are treated as an asset."

—**Mariana Castro**, Qualitative Research Director,
Multilingual Learning Research Center,
University of Wisconsin-Madison

"Some educators treat multilingual justice as an oxymoron, others envision multilingual justice as a belief system, still others embody multilingual justice as a way of being. In a carefully crafted and creative exposé, Honigsfeld artfully navigates the essential abilities of equity literacy to exemplify and sustain multilingual justice. In doing so, readers are captured by her poetic and personalized journey where, in becoming inculcated with multilingual justice, leads to taking action to transform the mindset and field of multilingual education."

—**Margo Gottlieb, PhD,** Co-founder, WIDA,
University of Wisconsin-Madison

"Andrea Honigsfeld brings both scholarly insight and deeply personal reflection to this powerful exploration of multilingual justice. Drawing on lived experience and research, she reminds us that language is never just about communication: it is about identity, dignity, and belonging. This book challenges educators to confront linguistic inequities while offering hopeful pathways toward more inclusive schools. A timely and essential reading for anyone committed to equity in multilingual education."

—**Luis Javier Pentón Herrera,** 2024 TESOL Teacher of the Year
and Professor at Uniwersytet VIZJA, Poland

"Dr. Honigsfeld positions language as identity, agency, and a fundamental right, not simply a tool for communication. What makes this work especially impactful is its clarity and usability: she defines multilingual justice in actionable ways across classrooms, systems, and policy contexts, while bridging Paul Gorski's equity literacy framework to the realities of multilingual learners. Reading this book, I felt deeply moved! The integration of personal narrative and rigorous scholarship is especially compelling. This work feels both human and immediately essential for educators and systems leaders seeking to enact meaningful, sustained change."

—**Melissa Lambert**, Executive Director, Office of Leadership and Engagement, Yonkers Public Schools, New York

"Multilingual students bring extraordinary gifts to our classrooms—gifts too often overlooked, dismissed, or silenced. In *Multilingual Justice in Schools*, Dr. Andrea Honigsfeld names this systemic harm while offering educators a clear and hopeful path forward. Courageous, practical, and deeply necessary, this book provides both inspiration and a roadmap for ensuring multilingual students can truly thrive."

—**Jennifer C. Mann, PhD,** Education Research Scientist, Center for Child and Family Policy, Duke University

"This book not only expresses a belief in language justice, it puts educators on a scholarly and practical path to expanding it. In this, Dr. Honigsfeld's work is not just powerful, it is vital to our work in school communities, and essential to our progress as a global society."

—**Cornelius Minor**, Educator and Bestselling Author

"Language rights are human rights. This axiom, contained in the Universal Declaration of Human Rights, is reinforced and amplified by Andrea Honigsfeld in this important new book. She shares what we can do to promote multilingualism and why it is important to respect the language rights of children who are learning English. She also reminds us that being literate in more than one language is an asset we should cultivate, and not something to be feared. For educators, parents, and anyone who sees language as a bridge that can unite humanity, this book will be a cherished resource."

—**Pedro A. Noguera, PhD,** Emery Stoops and Joyce King Stoops Dean, Rossier School of Education, University of Southern California

"Andrea Honigsfeld's heart-felt ode to multilingualism and the struggle for linguistic justice draws from a broad and deep network of researchers, educators and leaders. She has turned research into reflexivity and reflexivity into poetry, art, and resources. Educators, teacher educators, parents, community activists: if you are interested in expanding your toolkit, if you are interested in exploring the potential of multilingual languaging, I recommend this text for your next book-group circle."

—**Deb Palmer,** Professor of Equity, Bilingualism and Biliteracy, University of Colorado Boulder

"Andrea Honigsfeld has written a powerful and deeply necessary book for this moment in education and democracy. Multilingual justice is ultimately about whose voices are valued, whose identities are honored, and who gets to fully participate in schools and society. This book challenges educators to see multilingualism not as a deficit, but as dignity, belonging, agency, and strength. Courageous, timely, and deeply human."

—**Dr. Paul Bloomberg,** Best-Selling Author, *Metacognitive Clarity: Think Rigorously. Advance Democracy*

Multilingual Justice in Schools

Despite the growing number of multilingual learners in schools, there is bias surrounding the students and their families, and false assumptions that language differences mean a difference in academic ability.

In this important book, bestselling author Andrea Honigsfeld applies five essential abilities of equity literacy to multilingual justice, showing how to effectively work with multilingual learners while recognizing their strengths and identifying and addressing inequities and injustices they experience. The book provides educators with a concise, research-backed, and evidence-based analysis of *multilingual justice*, and offers practical and actionable recommendations to sustain equity for multilingual learners. It is a call to action to dismantle language-based inequities and injustices in our classrooms, schools, and larger educational communities.

Key features include poetry and art, authentic voices from the field; notable current research findings; ready-to-use tools and protocols; and time to pause and reflect. With this helpful resource, teachers, leaders, and teacher educators alike will feel equipped to bring about multilingual justice so their students can truly thrive.

Andrea Honigsfeld, EdD, is professor emerita in the School of Education and Human Services at Molloy University, Rockville Centre, New York, where she taught graduate courses related to cultural and linguistic diversity and TESOL methodology. She frequently offers professional learning opportunities, primarily focusing on effective content and language integration strategies and collaborative practices for ELD and bilingual/dual language specialists and general-education teachers. She has coauthored over 60 articles and chapters and coauthored or coedited over 35 books.

Equity and Social Justice in Education Series

Paul C. Gorski, Series Editor

Routledge's Equity and Social Justice in Education series is a publishing home for books that apply critical and transformative equity and social justice theories to the work of on-the-ground educators. Books in the series describe meaningful solutions to the racism, white supremacy, economic injustice, sexism, heterosexism, transphobia, ableism, neoliberalism, and other oppressive conditions that pervade schools and school districts.

Transformative Mindfulness in Education
Caring for Ourselves While Kindling Change
Rhiannon Kim

Teaching Indigenous Studies
An Introduction for K-12 Educators
Leilani Sabzalian, Meredith McCoy, and Helen Thomas

Peacebuilding Pedagogies
Racial Justice, Dialogue, and Belonging in the Classroom
Crystena Parker-Shandal

Cultivating Critical Advocacy
A Framework for Educators of Multilingual Learners
Rebecca E. Linares and Kate Seltzer

The DEI Practitioner's Handbook
A Guide for School and District Leaders in Pursuit of Educational Justice
Erica Buchanan-Rivera

Teaching Multilingual Learners in Rural Schools
Four Movements for Educators
Maria Coady

Healing-Centered Writing in the Secondary Classroom
An Identity-Affirming and Restorative Approach
Ioanna Pettas Opidee

Multilingual Justice in Schools
Centering Multilingual Learners' Academic, Linguistic, and Socio-Cultural Experiences
Andrea Honigsfeld

Identity-Conscious Teaching, Learning, and Curriculum
Strategies and Activities
Liza Talusan

Multilingual Justice in Schools

Centering Multilingual Learners' Academic, Linguistic, and Socio-Cultural Experiences

Andrea Honigsfeld

Routledge
Taylor & Francis Group
NEW YORK AND LONDON

Designed cover image: Getty Images

First published 2027
by Routledge
605 Third Avenue, New York, NY 10158

and by Routledge
4 Park Square, Milton Park, Abingdon, Oxon, OX14 4RN

Routledge is an imprint of the Taylor & Francis Group, an informa business

ISBN: 978-1-041-08167-8 (pbk)
ISBN: 978-1-003-64407-1 (ebk)

DOI: 10.4324/9781003644071

Typeset in Palatino
by KnowledgeWorks Global Ltd.

To all the members of, and advocates for, a just and equitable multilingual world

Contents

Foreword

I've visited hundreds of schools, mostly in North America. In each of these schools—some in generally progressive regions, others in more conservative areas—educators, leaders, and committees of educators and leaders are attending in various ways to matters of equity and justice. In a vast majority, the trouble is not so much the absence of equity efforts, even today, with all the anti-"DEI" sentiment and action. The trouble, as I see it, is that most of what schools do in the name of equity and justice tends toward minor actions and disconnected programs that do not make schools more equitable or just. Maybe they make conditions in classrooms and schools a smidge less xenophobic or racist with a little curriculum shift here, a dash of inclusiveness there, but they generally fall far short of addressing the root causes of inequities and disparities. I've come to refer to these sorts of equity efforts, the ones that nibble around inequity's edges but never quite manage to eliminate harmful conditions, as "high optics, low impact."

Conversations about equity in schools often are full of references to all manner of gaps: achievement gaps, reading gaps, preparedness gaps, opportunity gaps. But if we fail to address this other gap, the one between the core, underlying causes of disparities and the most popular, usually grossly inadequate responses to those causes, we have no real shot at making classrooms and schools more equitable. The most egregious misalignment of causes and responses often revolve around deficit presumptions. We, as a community of educators, sometimes seem preoccupied with finding fault with the most marginalized students and families and inventing solutions meant to adjust something about *them* rather than confronting the conditions that marginalize them.

Katy Swalwell and I conceived the equity literacy framework with this cause/response gap in mind. We constructed it around a series of values meant to push ourselves and fellow educators toward high impact equity and justice actions—actions like developing an anti-xenophobic, anti-racist curriculum rather than settling for minor tweaks and adjustments. We hoped educators might leverage it toward deeper, more serious change.

When Andrea Honigsfeld told me that she intended to build this book around my and Katy's equity literacy framework, leveraging some of its key components to champion equity and justice for multilingual learners, I was thrilled. I knew she had the equity chops and the transformative vision to apply the framework robustly. She's always been a fierce advocate for multilingual learners, her many previous books informed by an equity and justice ethic even when they weren't centrally focused on equity and justice. I knew she wouldn't disappoint. And she hasn't.

She frames this book around what Katy and I call the five abilities of equity literacy: the abilities to recognize even the subtlest inequity, to respond effectively in the moment we uncover inequity, to redress inequity as its root causes, to actively cultivate equity rather than only reacting to inequity, and to sustain equity efforts in the long term. By doing so she demonstrates how and why we need a comprehensive, student-voice-driven approach to advocating for multilingual learners. We need to attend to everyday classroom interactions. We must learn how to recognize all the insidious ways bias and inequity can creep into our spheres of influence despite our good intentions. We also must understand the bigger picture, how various forms of inequity intersect and interact, not just individually but institutionally. If we want the most profound change, we should be proactive cultivators of equity and justice rather than waiting to fix something after harm has occurred.

By stepping us through the abilities, Andrea broadens the possibilities for change. She widens our scope from the mitigative to the transformative, thereby deepening our potential impact. This is the spirit of the equity literacy framework, modeled more fully by Andrea in this book than in any other application I've ever witnessed or read. I'm both grateful and awed to see equity literacy applied with such depth and care.

Just as importantly, she invites us to engage with her, to be in conversation and reflection. Everything points toward growth, growth, growth. What a wonderful gift.

—Paul C. Gorski,
founder of the Equity Literacy Institute and
coauthor with Seema Pothini of *Case Studies on Diversity and Social Justice Education*, 3rd edition

Acknowledgements

I am forever indebted to the brilliant minds of the Delphi Panelists (see Appendix A for the complete list), and all other educators who shared their words of wisdom, their deepest beliefs and their advocacy stance with me. Engaging in deep conversations, reading your survey responses and emails, and learning from you along the way is a privilege I do not take lightly. I hope I have done justice to your contributions!

Margo Gottlieb and Audrey Cohan read earlier drafts of this manuscript. Your critical feedback, your affirmations, your mentorship and friendship have been precious gifts that I will always treasure.

A special thank you goes to the two amazing artists who generously worked on multiple versions of each illustration until we landed on the final ones you find on the pages of this book. Jacob Honigsfeld, a multilingual and multitalented chemistry major and art minor, who is also my son, drew the icons for the recurring chapter features. Colleen Wilcox, a brilliant Vermont-based lettering artist, captured the essence of each chapter with a black ink drawing embedded in the text.

I would like to thank the peer reviewers who offered their enthusiastic support for the proposal as well as valuable feedback on what they hope to see in this book and in the field of multilingual education.

Finally, I deeply appreciate the support of Paul Gorski and the entire Routledge editorial and production team. Paul has been a mentor to me, mostly from afar, whose work I have followed and built upon for many years. I cherished the opportunity to embrace an essential component of his equity literacy framework codeveloped with Katy Swalwell and apply the five abilities to multilingual justice in this book. Paul's powerful foreword is most appreciated!

1

Introduction

What is Language?

A tool to communicate
A thought to translate
A channel for cognition
A rich tapestry of expression
An incredible creation of collective art
A piece of my heart
An act of defiance
The opposite of silence
A vessel of history
A thread to memory

A part of my identity

Being multilingual is a beautiful, exhausting, uplifting, and overwhelming experience. At times, it is emotionally consuming and cognitively draining, yet at others it feels invigorating and spine-tinglingly thrilling. Yes, language use can do all that and so much more!

The sheer number of languages (close to 7150 according to Ethnologue, 2025) could take one's breath away. Indeed, the mere existence of so many languages has fascinated humankind from time immemorial resulting in several origin stories that identify language as a gift from God or other divine

DOI: 10.4324/9781003644071-1

origin. One of the most famous Judeo-Christian biblical stories speaks of the Tower of Babel, where once all the people of the Earth spoke one language and they decided to build a tower high enough to reach the heavens. Seeing such hubris and defiance, God brought his fury down to the people, confused their minds, made their speech unintelligible to each other, and if that had not been bad enough, dispersed them all over the world. I wonder what the unintended or underlying message might be: Is the multitude of languages a curse, a punishment, a divine consequence for courage and ingenuity?

In the Hindu tradition, a slightly similar scenario took place: when the Tree of Knowledge growing out of the center of the Earth began to reach heaven, the God Brahma intervened by cutting off and scattering the branches of the tree all over the world. Each branch turned into a new tree representing a new language and culture.

According to a Native American myth from the Yuki people in Southern California, Taikomol, the creator of the world, went on a long journey accompanied by Coyote. He created tribes in different locations by laying out sticks in the shape of people and gave them different customs and languages. Many origin myths focus on traveling or trickster gods spreading people across the Earth into different tribes with their own languages. Yet other stories explain the origins of so many languages by a desire to avoid conflict or to overcome a natural disaster.

After analyzing a range of myths, Przemysław Żywiczyński (2018) asserts that "language is special: it is not a human invention but a divine gift that distinguishes humans from other animals." He also highlights an "important idea found in mythological narratives is that the language of one's community, together with its customs and place of residence, constitutes one's second nature" (p. 28). Others, such as Leo van Lier and Aída Walqui, also suggest the importance of community when it comes to languages as they declare "language is an inseparable part of all human action, intimately connected to all other forms of action, physical, social and symbolic. Language is thus an expression of agency, embodied and embedded in the environment" (as cited in García, Kleifgen, & Cervantes-Soon, 2025, p. 99).

Pause for a Moment

Have you ever wondered about why there are so many languages? What is an origin story that you recall hearing or studying about? What is your core belief about where languages come from and the role they play in the lives of individuals and societies?

I have always been drawn to languages; in fact, I am venturing into studying my seventh language while I am working on this manuscript. The proverb my mother encouragingly passed on to me as a child, "Ahány nyelv, annyi ember" (You are as many people as many languages you speak), continues to affirm my passion for languages and commitment to multilingualism. Most recently, I have learned to embrace the notion of languaging, which refers to an action and an ongoing process rather than conceptualizing language as a static entity, a noun, or something that is finite and accomplished. As we engage in *languaging* or using language, we construct meaning, develop new understandings, articulate thoughts and feelings and engage in exchanges with others (Becker, 1991; Ernst-Slavit & Gottlieb, 2026; Swain, 2006).

Why do Languages, Languaging, and Multilingualism Matter?

Did you know ...?

- Over 40% of the 7000+ languages are endangered with less than 1000 speakers left.
- The 20 largest languages are spoken by 3.7 billion people.
- The top five most commonly spoken languages in the world are English, Mandarin Chinese, Hindi, Spanish, and Standard Arabic.
- There are between 350 and 430 languages spoken in the United States, of which over 170 are indigenous ones, making the US one of the most linguistically diverse countries in the world.
- According to the US census, in 2019, Spanish was the most common language spoken in US homes (62%) following English—12 times greater than the next four most common languages combined listed under Spanish (Chinese, Vietnamese, Korean, Tagalog) (American Community Survey, 2019).
- The United States did not have an official language until Executive Order 14224 was signed into law on March 1, 2025.

Statistics are much more than numbers; they tell a collective kind of story that helps to look at languages and multilingualism from the outside in. In this book, we are taking an inside-out perspective (centering lived experiences) and making *multi-languaging* personal and actionable.

Pause for a Moment

What fascinates you about languages?

What personal, familial or professional experiences do you have with multilingualism?

Why do languages and languaging matter in your professional context?

My personal story of multilingualism began in Hungary, studying multiple languages out of both necessity *and* joy! The national curriculum included the study of one compulsory foreign language (Russian) and one elective (my choice was English), but outside of school hours, I studied Italian with my sister, French with a friend and German on my own. My fight for my multilingualism, for my multilingual identity, and for multilingual justice for others found me many years later in the United States. More often than I would want to count, I was called out shortly after I opened my mouth when I first arrived in the United States and well … for a long time afterwards too! I was not called out for my bravery to speak in my third language, not for the ideas I was sharing, not for anything other than the detectable foreignness (ever so faint as many reassured me) of my speech:

"Where are you from?"

Often followed by a proclamation:

"I could not place your accent."

"You speak with just a slight inflection. It is more like a melody."

"You sound like my babysitter/aunt/neighbor _________ *[fill in the blank]*."

"Oh, my _______ [fill in the blank again] was born in Hungary, but I never learned the language. What a shame!"

Was it genuine interest?
Was it sincere curiosity?
Was it a form of compliment?
Is there an urgent, almost inevitable need to place, to compare, to identify when meeting someone for the first time?
Was it a way of othering and naming?
Was it an example of *the monolingual gaze,* simultaneously fascinated and annoyed by multilingualism?
When I was asked about the origin of my accent, the urge to give a different answer each time was tempting. Did it matter? To whom? And why?

The frequent curiosities, sometimes slipping into microaggressions, related to language difference followed me for many years! I was questioned about my sense of belonging, my identity, or even my loyalty, "So what are you really? A Hungarian American or an American Hungarian?" My dual citizenship and the torn sense of belonging of many first-generation immigrants formed a silent response inside: Both! Language and identity are closely intertwined for so many of us who speak more than one language, belong to more than one land, embrace more than one national or ethnic identity.

When my first child was born, we lived in one of the most linguistically and culturally diverse neighborhoods in the entire United States, the borough of Queens, New York City. I was sure that multilingualism would be the norm. I heard and appreciated so many languages around me! It was only natural that I cooed and sang in Hungarian, fully committed to raising my children bilingually. Yet, when my first baby was only a few months old, a trip to the local park gave me a rude awakening. I was happily chatting with my son, in Hungarian, as my language of choice and language of affection, when an elderly woman sitting on the bench near us turned to me to firmly remind me:

"You are in America now, teach your child English!"

I had no response. Silence grew inside me again! I had not found my voice to call for acceptance, appreciation, or multilingual justice yet!

One day when my children had playdates in our home, I overheard a conversation about me. I was surprised and delighted to hear my then 7-year-old fiercely defending me, "No, my mother does not speak with an accent!" He did not hear it, or it did not bother him! Or maybe his 7-year-old self simply knew better, he did not want it to matter to him or anyone else!

Multilingualism cannot be separated from multicultural identities, linguistic pluralism, and the immigrant experience: What is being acknowledged, celebrated, valued, *or not* by individuals, schools, communities, and larger societies? As I also learned early on, my multilingualism is a form of white privilege, so many admiring my capacity and experiences with languages rather than seeing it is a deficit. Not all languages, not all varieties of languages, and not everyone's bilingualism and multilingualism are appreciated the same way, which must be acknowledged and confronted!

Tapestry of Voices

Ester de Jong, Professor in the Culturally and Linguistically Diverse Education program, at the University of Colorado, Denver, cautions about the need to explicitly discuss whose languages and which language varieties are valued:

> *There are linguistic hierarchies that make certain kinds of multilingualism more valuable than others. Within our discussion of multilingualism being a value, we also have to have a real conversation around whether we truly mean this for all languages, or only for prestigious languages, or only for standard forms of the language? This needs to be discussed very explicitly to avoid double standards.*

My plight and fight for multilingual justice, which began as something deeply personal, continue to be both professional and political. I share the passionate commitment expressed in Katrin Kohl and Wen-chin Ouyang's (2020) multilingual manifesto, which goes like this: "The entitlement of individuals and cultural groups to express themselves in their distinctive language must be supported as a fundamental human right and must be nurtured as vital to the sustainability of the natural and cultural world" (p. 1). Furthermore, let us also acknowledge that all members of language communities have access to a diverse array of linguistic resources, including language varieties and dialects, collectively referred to as their full linguistic repertoires.

Tapestry of Voices

Diep Nguyen, President and Chief Executive Officer of the Center for Applied Linguistics, also confirmed the need to broaden our perspective on multilingual justice:

> *One of the most fundamental parts of linguistic justice that we can't ignore is the fact that linguistic or language rights are human rights first and foremost, I think fundamentally, it is about a human right that we need to protect and that we need to ensure that it is respected for everyone.*

Ying Chu, Director of Chinese and Dual Language Learning, International School of Beijing, China, offers a unique perspective of why achieving multilingual justice is a global challenge:

> *In international schools (English medium schools in non-English speaking countries), the legacy of linguistic and cultural inequity is deeply rooted in the very core of the so-called international education, whether it is parents' internalized oppression demonstrated as the over-emphasis of learning English and the Western culture, or the dominant western structures, perspectives, power and privilege at play, or the curricular, assessment, and pedagogical approaches. It is disheartening. A few approaches we would advocate for are: implementing dual language bilingual programs to provide access to multilingual educational programs, establishing equitable language policies to institutionalize practices, and leadership and teachers' linguistic background should respond to that of the students and families; disrupting "English as the power of language" ideology and reality in international schools to redefine what is international education.*

Pause for a Moment

Do you have a favorite motto or manifesto as an educator?
What is your linguistic or multilingual motto or manifesto as an educator?
Why should language rights be considered human rights?

Some Key Definitions

Languaging is powerful. How we use words may simultaneously shape and reflect our thinking at any given time or any given topic. For example, how we string words together to formulate a simple definition will depend on our beliefs, experiences, conscious and unconscious thought processes and much more. Do you mean what I mean when I say "multilingual"? Do we see eye to eye regarding what defines justice? Will our definitions rely on the same experiential base and belief system? What are some myths or misconceptions out there that need to be addressed by achieving clarity around some basic terms?

For the sake of this book, defining multilingualism and multilingual learners seems to have been a relatively straightforward task. Tapping into decades of research and contemporary perspectives, I propose the following working definitions.

Multilingualism

Multilingualism is the ability to use more than one language, which may be considered a phenomenon at the individual, institutional, or societal levels.

- The *individual trait* refers to having the skills and competences to employ multiple languages for communicative purposes across a variety of contexts.
- *Institutional multilingualism* recognizes that multiple languages are being used within the context of an organization.
- *Societal multilingualism* acknowledges that multiple languages are being used within a country or region for personal or official purposes.

Multilingualism does not suggest full competence or fluency in all languages involved; indeed, most multilingual individuals or entities demonstrate varied levels of interpretive (formerly known is receptive skills) or expressive (also known is productive skills) for a given topic, situation, and audience.

Tapestry of Voices

Nury Castillo Crawford, Past President of the Georgia Association of Latino Administrators and Superintendents and celebrated bilingual children's book author, shares the essence of being bilingual or multilingual as follows:

> *Having another language feels like carrying a second soul within you. It shapes how you think, feel, and connect with others. For me, language isn't just words—it's identity, culture, and belonging.*

Ceci Gomez-Galvez (she, her, ella), collaborator, coach, and advocate, also highlights the importance of languages being connected to identity.

> *I lead with the belief that language is deeply tied to dignity. Every time we restrict how multilingual students can communicate, we limit their access to joy, agency, and rigorous learning. Equity work asks us to listen closely to students, learn from their linguistic creativity, and challenge policies that confuse sameness with fairness. When we center multilingualism, we move closer to schools that truly belong to everyone.*

Multilingual Learners

I will define multilingual learners as B-20 (from birth to college) students who have emerging language and literacy skills in more than one language. This definition will embrace bilingual and bidialectal students as well. By virtue of recognizing multilingualism as a powerful trait in these learners, I will use an asset-based terminology positioning students as knowers rather than highlighting what is lacking or missing. I will use multilingual learners to be the most inclusive term possible even if in some other contexts some of the same students would be referred to as English learners, Emergent Bilinguals, Multilingual Learners of English, or Emergent Multilingual Learners.

Multilingual Justice

While this entire book is designed to unpack what multilingual justice is and how to ensure it is enacted in classrooms, schools, districts, and communities, here is a working definition with some elaboration. I worked with a panel of internationally recognized experts on multilingualism to come to some definitions, using a variation of the Delphi approach (RAND, 2025). I created a modified protocol of this most intriguing qualitative research method.

I assembled a panel of internationally recognized experts on multilingualism and invited them to participate in two rounds of surveys and either in a focus group discussion or an individual interview as a final step in the process. See Appendix A for more details on the Delphi approach and the acknowledgement page for the members of the panel. After synthesizing the expert opinions I gathered, the definition of multilingual justice and multilingual injustice that emerged from the process are as follows. These are not perfect, finite, irrevocable understandings; yet they offer the clarity needed for this book to unfold and the complexity that allows room to grow and explore:

> Multilingual justice is the recognition, valuing, and support of all languages and language varieties as fundamental components of both individual, intergenerational, and collective identity. It ensures equitable access to rights, resources, and opportunities regardless of the language a person speaks, while rejecting language as a tool for exclusion, discrimination, or unearned privilege. Multilingual justice means that multilingual individuals have the freedom to use their entire linguistic repertoire across all contexts (such as health care, education, civic life, judicial system) without having to shed any part of who they are with their intersectional identities and learner agency. It challenges language hierarchies by recognizing students' home languages as assets, not deficits, and ensures that language minoritized individuals are not discriminated against based on their language.

Pause for a Moment

What are the first thoughts that come to mind as you finish reading this definition?

Did you have to reread some parts a second time and pause to reflect on the severity of these ideas?

Did some parts resonate with you more than others and why?

What might you still add to this definition?

If you are pondering what all this really means in the educational context, I am ready to unpack it with you. Let's move this definition into our classrooms, schools, districts, and communities and agree to the following. To achieve multilingual justice, we must:

- Recognize and value our multilingual students and all multilingual members of our community as assets, not liabilities and problems riddled with deficits.

- Engage multilingual families in their children's education through accessible communication, interpretation, translation services, and participation in decision-making processes. Multilingual justice goes beyond document translation—it ensures that families are informed, empowered, and seen as partners.
- Create multilingual programming as high-impact approaches that honor and sustain students' home languages, while also promoting academic achievement and biliteracy or multiliteracy.
- Design and implement culturally and linguistically responsive curricula and instruction that reflect students' languages, identities, and cultural experiences.
- Apply teaching strategies that affirm students' backgrounds, avoid tokenism, and position learners as co-creators of knowledge—ensuring their cultural and linguistic lived experiences, including all varieties of Englishes shape classroom learning.
- Utilize assessment practices that are fair, multimodal, accessible, and designed to accurately reflect students' understanding and growth in all of their languages—not just the dominant one.
- Build educators' capacity to view multilingualism as a strength. This includes shifting from deficit-based thinking to asset-oriented practices, and ensuring that teachers receive ongoing, in-depth professional learning opportunities on supporting multilingual learners effectively.

How do we achieve all this? Well, that is what the rest of this book is about, but first things first. We should also define multilingual injustice. The definition that the Delphi panel agreed on sounds like this:

> Multilingual injustice is the systemic exclusion, marginalization, or harm inflicted on individuals or communities due to their linguistic backgrounds. It occurs when educational systems privilege dominant languages—especially English—while rejecting, devaluing, or suppressing the home languages of multilingual learners. This injustice manifests through linguistically biased assessments, exclusionary policies, denial of support services, and a failure to recognize the cultural and cognitive assets of multilingualism. Linguistic discrimination is often connected to racial and other forms of discrimination (e.g., using language as a proxy for race). It restricts access to equitable learning, silences student identities, limits participation, and perpetuates social and educational hierarchies. Whether intentional or unintentional,

multilingual injustice denies learners their right to thrive academically, culturally, and personally by framing their languages as deficits rather than strengths.

Pause for a Moment

Was your thinking affirmed by any parts of this definition? What have you found the most startling and eye opening? What might be you add to this definition from your own experience?

Throughout the chapters, look for special featured boxes for select quotes from the Delphi panelists and other experts in the field; their words of wisdom will enrich the message I craft in the forthcoming chapters.

Standing on Giants' Shoulders

Both empirical and conceptual work that addresses language justice, linguistic justice, language for social justice, and some other critical resources have been published prior to this book, inspired me, and challenged me to build upon them. Among many others, Ingrid Piller (2016, 2021) focuses on social justice and linguistic diversity as she meticulously analyzes how global migration and economic inequality lead to linguistic subordination. Connecting language, linguistics, and justice has been expertly accomplished by April Baker-Bell (2020), who offers counter stories of Black students' identities to dismantle *anti-Black linguistic racism* often manifested as the dehumanization and marginalization of Black Language-speakers.

With a social justice focus and emphasis on *raciolinguistics*, also explored by Nelson Flores (2020, 2024), H. Samy Alim et al.'s (2020) edited volume sheds further light on the complex relationships between and among race, ethnicity, and language. In another academic collection of edited chapters, Lydia Liu and Anupama Rao with Charlotte Silverman (2024) weave together a range of perspectives on global issues related to language loss and linguistic diversity with the goal of safeguarding marginalized and endangered languages. Netta Avineri and Patricia Baquedano-López (2024) investigate the intersectionality of language, inequality, and social justice and explore the past, present, and future of language and social justice issues (LJSIs). A recently established journal, *Racial Justice in Multilingual Education*, underscores the expanding interest in and need for this specialized line of scholarship. A most current volume edited by Luciana de Oliveira and Karen Terrell (2026) offers a carefully curated line up of chapters uncovering ways to prepare antiracist ESOL (English to Speakers of Other Languages) professionals to ensure linguistic equity for multilingual learners. There are many more resources that I will be citing and quoting throughout the forthcoming pages making explicit connections to both contemporary and seminal work.

Notable Research

For a growing number of researchers, studying and advocating for equity for multilingual learners have become a focus point. In the introduction to their edited volume consisting of a comprehensive selection of teacher action research studies, Meg Gebhard and Kathryn Accurso, emphasize the need for pursuing a multilingual equity agenda:

> *A multilingual equity agenda focuses squarely on students who have historically been marginalized in school, especially those whose language practices have been racialized or otherwise stigmatized as a result of deficit ideologies, institutional racism, and deskilling approaches to teaching. Chief among the ideologies this agenda challenges are:*
>
> - *Unexamined beliefs about language and grammar*
> - *Misguided commitments to English monolingualism and the supremacy of national varieties of written language*
> - *Deficit thinking regarding the academic abilities of students officially designated as "English language learners" (ELLs), especially those of color*
> - *The belief that student learning and teacher professional development are primary individual accomplishments as opposed to collective activities that require sustained institutional investments and political will.*
>
> (Gebhard & Accurso, 2023, p. 3)

The Purpose

This book is designed to center multilingualism in the equity discourse within the *Equity and Social Justice in Education* series. It focuses on a less commonly explored topic—***multilingual justice.*** It fits well among other books in the series that address racism, white supremacy, economic injustice, sexism, hetero-sexism, transphobia, ableism, neoliberalism, and other oppressive conditions that pervade schools, school districts, and society while it also provides a much-needed new, justice-seeking dimension of equity work.

I first set out to explore the transferability of Paul Gorski's (n.d.) equity literacy framework to multilingual learners and multilingualism several years ago and found a powerful possibility to make meaningful connections. To clarify upfront, this is not a book on literacy for multilingual learners. Equity literacy is defined as a comprehensive approach that

> *prepares us to recognize even the subtlest forms of bias, inequity, and oppression related to race, class, gender identity and expression, sexual orientation, (dis)ability, language, religion, immigration status, and other factors. Through equity literacy we prepare ourselves to understand how we experience disparities, not just quantitatively measured outcome disparities, affect student access to equitable educational opportunity free of bias, inequity, and discrimination.*
>
> (Gorski, n.d., para. 2)

The main purpose of this book is to systematically apply the five essential abilities of *equity literacy* to multilingual justice. According to Paul Gorski and Katy Swalwell (2023a), these abilities are to accomplish the following:

1. Recognizing even the subtlest biases and inequities.
2. Responding skillfully and equitably to biases and inequities in the immediate term.
3. Redressing biases and inequities by understanding and addressing them at their institutional roots.
4. Actively cultivating equity by applying an equity commitment to every decision.
5. Sustaining equity efforts even in the face of discomfort or resistance.

The overarching intent for the book is to provide educators with a concise, research-backed, and evidence-based analysis of *multilingual justice* and to make practical and actionable recommendations to sustain multilingual justice. I wish to unapologetically recognize the every-day, ordinary genius and the often untapped, exceptional giftedness of multilingualism and why we all need to dismantle language-based inequities and injustices in our classrooms, schools, and larger educational communities.

Tapestry of Voices

Margo Gottlieb, Cofounder and Lead Developer of WIDA at the University of Wisconsin-Madison, offers her asset-based perspective of multilingual justice as follows:

To me multilingual justice is equated with human dignity. Being human means being just, fair, and egalitarian. Multilingual justice entails the wonders of the world and for myself and many others, being multilingual and multicultural. Ultimately, multilingual justice is respecting each and every person as an individual and embracing all their being—their beauties, their languages, and their cultures.

Pause for a Moment

What is your intention with reading this book?
What are your short-term and long-term goals to achieve linguistic justice?

The Organization

The book consists of six chapters and an Epilogue. The Foreword was written by Paul Gorski, who offers a brief background to his equity literacy framework and why and how this volume provides a viable expansion of it.

Chapter 1: Introduction

The introductory chapter is designed to set the tone for the entire book. I offer a brief overview of the goals of the book, as well as establish what this short volume is set out to accomplish and what is beyond its scope. I answer some key questions right away to pique the interest of the reader such as (but not limited to):

- What are the origins of language justice?
- Who are multilingual learners and members of our immediate and larger communities and their connections to multilingual justice?

- Why is it imperative to dismantle inequities and injustices that multilingual learners and their families experience?
- Who is this book for and what contribution does it make?
- How is the book going to accomplish its ambitious goals?

I preview the forthcoming chapters aligned to the five abilities of equity literacy (Gorski & Swalwell, 2023a) and introduce the recurring features of the book with examples to provide a feel for what you will experience in the rest of the book.

Chapter 2: How to Recognize Multilingual Inequities and Injustices

In this chapter, my goal is to address the first ability in the equity literacy framework, recognizing inequities and injustices in multilingual education and multilingual learners. I intend to raise awareness about what types of subtle or not so subtle (occasionally outright blatant and explicit) *deficit-oriented* perspectives, ideologies, policies and practices exist in classrooms, schools, and larger school communities that multilingual learners and their families encounter.

The focus of the chapter is on how to develop the ability to become aware of, spot, recognize, identify, and name the kinds of misconceptions, biases, microaggressions, and/or oppressive beliefs that members of a school community may have about multilingualism and may hold against multilingual students. I also provide guidance on how to identify and acknowledge the harm that deficiency perspectives cause and how to discern and develop an assets-based lens to multilingualism and multilingual learners. In addition, I note high-impact equity practices to help educators intentionally look for examples of inequities through critical actions and reflection individually or with collegial support.

Chapter 3: How to Respond to Multilingual Inequities and Injustices

In this chapter, I align the second ability in the equity literacy framework, responding to inequities and injustices, to multilingualism and multilingual learners. The goal of this chapter is to explore multidimensional opportunities for immediate or shorter-term responses to multilingual inequities and injustices that are not merely recognized but addressed in the moment as well.

First, I unpack Ricardo Ruíz's original tri-part policy framework of viewing language as a problem, right or resource and apply it to multilingualism by offering examples and discussing the implications of each. I categorize immediate or short-term responses to multilingual inequities and injustices as ones that may take place in words or in actions and explore successful practices that go beyond these token acknowledgements—celebrating Hispanic Heritage Month or Asian American Pacific Islander Heritage for a designated time of the year, acknowledging International Mother Language Day or National Bilingual/Multilingual Learner Advocacy Month and so on. The chapter will help foster difficult conversations about preconceived notions and prejudices that may exist in a number of places, such as in long-held ideologies or mental models. It will also identify practical, actionable strategies that respond to inequities and injustices immediately or in the shorter term.

Chapter 4: How to Redress Multilingual Inequities and Injustices

In this chapter, I align the third ability in the equity literacy framework, redressing inequities, to multilingualism and multilingual learners. The goal of the chapter is to help develop educators' capacity to commit to long-term actions in response to multilingual inequities and injustices. These include removing all educational experiences and barriers that are limiting and detrimental to multilingual learners' opportunities and ensuring that they, too, can thrive and fully demonstrate their abilities to achieve at the highest possible levels, including continuing to develop their multilingualism and multiliteracies.

I accomplish this by presenting ways to (a) not only identify the underlying causes of the biases and oppressive ideologies that surround multilingualism and multilingual learners but to eliminate them, (b) connect these inequities to school and district level policies and practices that favor monolingual, standard and standardized language and literacy practices, and (c) outline what needs to be done to revamp curricular, instructional and assessment practices. This chapter shifts from merely identifying and responding to individual examples of inequitable practices that typically take place in personal encounters or during classroom level interactions to proactively advocating for rectifying persistent harms that multilingual learners may experience as well as amending them with new policies and practices at the school level.

Chapter 5: How to Cultivate Multilingual Equity and Justice

In this chapter, I align the fourth ability in the equity literacy framework—cultivating equity and justice—to multilingualism and multilingual learners. There is a marked shift in this chapter as suggested by the title: my focus is on exploring ways to *actively utilize an equity lens to everything* that multilingual learners experience from the moment they arrive on our schools' doorsteps to the day they graduate from high school and beyond, including but not limited to:

- Processes that are put in place to identify and place multilingual learners in programs without over-, under-, or misidentification.
- The legal obligations schools and districts have to protect the rights of students designated as English language learners.
- The development of equitable Lau Plans and the implementation of language development programs that fully honor multilingualism.
- The collaborative culture of equity and justice that educators jointly build into their classrooms, schools, and larger communities, with close attention to family and community engagement.

The chapter offers not one but two "spotlight" case studies to provide additional authentic examples from the field.

Chapter 6: How to Sustain Multilingual Equity and Justice

In this ambitious last chapter, I align the final ability in the equity literacy framework to multilingualism and multilingual learners. I express a sincere hope for a bright future in which we have already recognized, responded to, redressed and cultivated equity for multilingual justice and explore how to sustain the work! I urgently call for action to make equitable classrooms, schools and districts for multilingualism the norm through sustained, ongoing commitment to equity and by taking actionable steps that lead to lasting justice for multilingual learners. Sustaining multilingual equity and justice requires a close examination of district, school and departmental values and policies regarding multilingualism, re-envisioning institutional priorities when it comes to resources, hiring and staffing decisions, and ongoing professional learning. I acknowledge that there are numerous challenges and many possible forms of resistance to fully accepting multilingual learners in the school and district communities, and I map out what different members of a school community can do! My hope is that the work to make our schools linguistically just and equitable is deemed meaningful, aspirational, yet achievable.

Epilogue

I close the volume with one more poem I wrote to bring the entire book together in an encouraging way to continue our equity work.

Tapestry of Voices

Wayne E. Wright, Associate Dean for Research, Graduate Programs, and Faculty Development, Professor and Barbara I. Cook Chair of Literacy and Language College of Education, Purdue University, West Lafayette, Indiana, offers his perspective of why multilingual equity and justice matter:

I really like the term multilingual justice! Language diversity means there's more than one language besides English in the world, like 7000 others, and social justice means people should be able to learn, teach and use them. That doesn't seem that radical to me!

I conducted a study on the personal impact of the English-only policies on individuals, particularly students: when they go through our education system that erases their bilingualism that they started school with, they talk about their struggles and their challenges, even getting their parents to understand them and having to have someone interpret between them and their parents.

There is also a disconnect between our language education policy that tends to erase bilingual learners' resources and the critical need we have for multilingual people in the education sector, in the diplomatic sector, in the defense sector, in the commerce sector, in the tourism sector; it's just a huge disconnect. When we talk about justice, it's not just for individuals, but really what's good for society as a whole. And I think that's what's lost when we don't pay attention to multilingual justice.

This book is for you …

- ◆ If you are new to social justice education.
- ◆ If you have had prior experience with social justice education but wish to center the multilingual learners.
- ◆ If you are new to multilingual education.
- ◆ If you are familiar with an asset-based approach to supporting multilingual learners but need more specific pathways to social justice.

The book is intended for B-20 practitioners, educators, teacher educators, college professors, graduate students, policy makers, and others interested in multilingualism as a human right and social justice issue.

Tapestry of Voices

Tanya Rosado-Barringer, ENL Director, Department of Bilingual Education and World Languages, Rochester City School District, New York, highlights the importance of recognizing equity work as a long-term professional commitment. Educators do not have to be bilingual or multilingual themselves to be the strongest advocates for multilingualism as demonstrated by her message:

> *As a monolingual leader on a lifelong journey toward bilingualism, I have had to unpack internalized bias and reframe my lens to honor the deep cultural and linguistic wealth of the communities I serve. Across all my professional roles, I have remained focused in designing systems that elevate multilingual learners from the margins to the center. Multilingual justice means co-constructing pathways that affirm identity, restore linguistic dignity, and position students' home languages as powerful assets in their lifelong learning journeys.*

Noteworthy Features

There will be multiple unique elements that provide either an extension or an enrichment of each chapter. Look out for the following recurring chapter features:

- **Poetry**—to take a poetic view of complex issues related to the topic of each chapter written by the author, Andrea.
- **A Tapestry of Voices**—to hear from members of the Delphi Panel, researchers, leaders and educators in B-20 school contexts.
- **Pause for a Moment**—to engage in critical reflections on each major section of a chapter.
- **Notable Research**—to present research findings and quotes from seminal and current studies and undergird the message in the text.
- **Illustrations**—to add visual support for key points made in the chapter.
- **Tools and Protocols**—to consider some practical tools and protocols and to help find evidence of each equity literacy ability for multilingual learners and multilingualism.
- **Spotlights on Equity—**to showcase successful examples of multilingual equity and justice as mini case studies reported by educators from around the United States.
- **Lettering Arts**—to provide visual representations of select concepts or ideas through artistic expressions by Colleen Wilcox.

LANGUE
SPROG
TEANGA
JEZYK
NGÔN NGỮ
KIELI
語言
LANGUAGES
SPRACHE
NYELV
LINGUA
ʻŌLELO
KEEL
LLENGUA
IDIOMA
لغة
زبان
TAAL
ZIMAN
BAHASA
भाषा
VALODA
LÍNGUA
SPRÅK
мова
dil
IK
ULIMI
CHINENERO
IAITH

End-of-Chapter Reflections

Before you set out on this exploration with me, reflect on the following:

★ What does multilingualism mean to you personally, professionally, politically?
★ How does linguistic justice fit into equity work in your context?
★ What works in your immediate and broader educational community and what should be done to further multilingual justice?

2

How to Recognize Multilingual Inequities and Injustices

What Can Be

Can language be a means of exclusion?
Can it be a tool of discrimination?
Who can be at an advantage?
What can be the cost of a linguistic disadvantage?

Going for a Walk

Come and take a walk with me!

Let's enter a few classrooms, step into a school library, and stay a bit in the gym.

What languages do you hear spoken? What resources are available in English and in any other languages to the students? Are speakers of the same languages (other than English) sitting together?

Let's walk the hallways, linger in the lunchroom, and venture into the school yard.

What are some snippets of conversations that you catch among students, students and their caregivers, and among guardians? What quick exchanges do you catch at arrival or dismissal times?

DOI: 10.4324/9781003644071-2

Let's take a quick peek into the main office, the teachers' lounge, or the conference room.

What is being discussed about students who speak languages other than English?

Let's visit a soccer practice, stop by a band and choir rehearsal, or hang out in the afterschool center.

Who is doing most of the talking and in what language(s)?

Let's pop into a parent-teacher conference, participate in some after-school events, or attend a school board meeting.

Are there translators or interpreters available? Does everyone in the room understand what is being said? Who does all or most of the talking? Is everyone's voice heard?

Take this imaginary walking tour a step further (no pun intended) and walk around your school community paying attention to all the languages, language varieties and dialects. Sarah Ottow (2023) frequently discusses the use of a *language lens,* which helps educators think about how language occurs in the curriculum, "what challenges students may have," and how to "provide appropriate support and knowledge to plan explicit language goals" (p. 18). We will revisit this concept in Chapter 4, where we explore an integrated approach to content and language development. Here, I am inviting you to use a *linguistic lens,* which will help focus on listening for every-day and academic conversations, noticing languages, watching human interactions taking place, and observing linguistic expectations, norms, and authentic behaviors.

Whether you joined me on the fictitious stroll that might have triggered some long-lost memories or brought back more recent experiences, or if you took the time to turn a walk around your building into a more intentional listening tour, I invite you to think back to your observations:

- What languages were used, valued, accepted, or merely tolerated in your school?
- What languages were frowned upon, dismissed, or missing from these spaces? Have you noticed interruptions, silenced conversations, or the absence of some languages you anticipated encountering?
- If you caught any conversations about languages or those who were interacting in multiple languages, what was being discussed?
- What languages were visibly on display? What did you see on the walls, near entrances, on bulletin boards or in some common areas such as offices and restrooms?

This was merely a quick walk, an initial opportunity to tune into the linguistic landscape of your school or larger local educational context. Soon, we will explore some more structured, intentional ways to notice and note what multilingual inequities might look like, sounds like, and feel like, so keep those walking shoes handy and your ears and eyes ready to take more in!

Before we move on, let's agree that languages cannot be separated from those who speak them, embrace them, honor them as an important part of their identities. So, think about the multilingual learners, their immediate or extended family members, multilingual staff or faculty, or other participants of the immediate or larger school community as you consider these questions:

- Are multilingual learners being acknowledged for their assets, gifts, and talents?
- Are they heard, seen, and valued?
- Has anyone in the school community ever been asked not to speak their home language?
- Has anyone in the school community ever felt that they cannot or should not speak their home language?
- Are multilingual members of the community known or noted for deficits and deficiencies in their language, in their understanding, in their experiential past, and what they bring to the school community?

I invite you to jot down some notes in the margins of the book and return to them later.

Tapestry of Voices

Deborah Short, founder and director of, Academic Language Research & Training, former division director at the Center for Applied Linguistics (CAL), reminds us to take a historical, more nuanced perspective of why and how multilingual justice and injustice have changed:

> *Our understanding of multilingual justice has evolved over the decades, particularly as we have had opportunities to hear and understand the stories of people marginalized for their language/cultural backgrounds and as the field of second language acquisition (SLA) has revealed more about the value of translanguaging. We are more informed now about better practices. There is a range of behavioral intents we should acknowledge. Not all multilingual injustices came from a "bad" place. Some practices occurred with good intentions, some from ignorance. Some though were more deliberate efforts to be disrespectful or to consolidate power and control. When we know about the motivations behind the injustice, we can take more appropriate action.*

Recognizing Linguistic Inequities

The first ability to build a robust capacity for multilingual justice is one's ability to ***recognize*** even the subtlest biases, inequities, and oppressive ideologies. According to Paul Gorski and Katy Swalwell (2023a), this ability translates into:

- noticing bias in learning materials and classroom interactions;
- developing curiosity about how school policies and practices disadvantage some students (be it intentional or unintentional); and
- rejecting deficit ideology and understanding that outcome disparities are not caused by the students coming from marginalized communities but many other complex factors.

They also note that cultivating this first ability is essential to future success: "If we fail to develop and practice [the ability to recognize inequity] the other abilities don't matter; we are doomed to perpetuate inequity" (Gorski & Swalwell, 2023a, p. 47). So, let's make a commitment to start off strong and intentionally work on recognizing inequities that are directly connected to multilingualism and multilingual identities.

What Does it Mean to Recognize Multilingual Inequities and Injustices?

You recognize multilingual inequities and injustices, when you notice

- whose language is visible and audible;
- what language is valued when used for personal and professional purposes;
- what languages are available for whom, when, and where;
- who gets to communicate with ease and with whom;
- who has access to information because there are no language barriers; and
- that language is integral to one's identity.

Barriers to Recognizing Multilingual Inequities and Injustice

There are many reasons inequities and injustices related to linguistic diversity are hard to spot. If you are a monolingual speaker of the dominant language (it is English in the United States) and most of your personal and professional experiences are primarily connected to the language that is privileged by society, it might be more challenging to recognize inequities and injustices. When monolingualism rules, the dominant language becomes the norm and, as such, invisible to those who can readily access it, and use it without even giving it a second thought. It is all around us, just like the famous parable about the fish that does not know it is swimming in water because it is oblivious to its natural surroundings. If the norms and expectations are that English is to be utilized for all educational purposes by all members of the school community at all times, those who have proficiency with it—whether as their mother tongue or as an additional language in which they have developed capacity—are more likely to overlook or not be cognizant of language-based inequities. When we live with the certainty and safety of understanding everything around us and communicating with ease across varied personal contexts, we are likely to bring our linguistically privileged identities to our professional lives in our schools and classrooms, intentional equity work is even more important.

Tapestry of Voices

Andrea Hellman, Professor of Linguistics/TESOL at Missouri State University, agrees that recognition represents the most urgent need in our schools today when addressing multilingual justice.

Before implementing any equity literacy framework for multilingual justice, educational institutions must first cultivate a genuine willingness among staff to examine existing practices for language-based biases, a foundation more fundamental than the technical ability to recognize inequities. This crucial first step requires creating psychologically safe spaces where educators can acknowledge how language hierarchies might be operating in their classrooms without feeling their professional identities are under attack. Leadership should model this vulnerability by openly sharing their own learning journeys with language bias, framing recognition not as finding fault but as expanding awareness to better serve all students. When this willingness is authentically developed through thoughtful community-building, educators become receptive to the deeper work of recognition, enabling them to see previously invisible patterns of multilingual injustice that their good intentions alone could not reveal, ultimately creating the necessary conditions for meaningful transformation toward language equity.

Paul Gorski and Katy Swalwell (2023b) call us to stay alert, develop critical consciousness around inequities, and make it a habit to notice them. Their unapologetic warning about injustices is a call to early action: "the question is not *whether* they exist. Injustice is *always* operating; it's embedded in policies, unexamined practices, traditions. Practice recognizing it until doing so becomes second nature" (p. 22). In this chapter, we are going to do just that. First, we take some initial steps to look inward and then explore more complex practices that lead to fully recognizing multilingual inequities and injustices, while acknowledging that awareness raising and deepened understanding of inequities will need to be followed by actions.

> **Pause for a Moment**
>
> In your own experience, what examples come to mind when you noticed multilingual inequities and injustices connected to multilingualism or multilingual students and other members of your school community?
>
> What or who helped you become aware of them?
>
> What were your reactions?

Taking Action to Recognize Multilingual Inequities and Injustices

Before

Look and see what was not apparent before
Listen and hear whose voices were muffled or ignored before
Watch and notice what was merely a blur on the periphery before
Read and note what fell to the margins before

Getting Started with Confronting Some Misconceptions and Recognizing Our Own Biases

First things first! How about we begin with the most personal aspect of equity literacy work, our own core beliefs about multilingualism, our own biases and misconceptions? In Chapter 1, I shared some origin stories and myths about how languages have evolved, now it is your turn! I invite you to consider the following ten statements and identify whether they are myths or facts.

Myths or Facts?

1. Introducing a second language during infancy will lead to cognitive delays.
2. Young children are like sponges; they just pick up any language they get exposed to.
3. School-age children get confused and mix languages when they are exposed to more than one language at a time.
4. Once you hit a certain age (around puberty), acquiring a second language with "native-like fluency" will not be possible.

5 Parents should stop speaking their home language(s) to their children, especially if students experience learning difficulties.
6 Trying to learn two or more languages at the same time will hinder core academic learning.
7 Bilingualism or multilingualism will lead to problems.
8 Bilingual education is ineffective; students in the US must be exposed to English instruction as soon as possible.
9 Multilingual learners should develop advanced English language skills before they can successfully participate in grade-level core content learning.
10 Some languages or varieties of languages are not as sophisticated as others for communication and we must prevent our students from learning "bad or poor English."

(Turn to Appendix B at the end of the book to check for correct answers and some relevant resources to further explore the professional literature about these statements.)

There is an abundance of myths and commonly held misconceptions, I could have listed 20 or 30 easily. Some of the phrases I inserted into these ten claims also indicate deep-rooted biases connected to age-differences in language acquisition and the misunderstood goal of multilingualism to become a "balanced bilingual" with "perfect English." These beliefs do more harm than good to both students and their families. Many outdated concepts or myths are shared even by well-meaning educators, who, with the best of intention, might offer misguided advice to multilingual families. I have experienced a fair share of this with my three children, the most memorable one was when my youngest child was experiencing processing difficulties, and we received an early intervention referral in his preschool. After several tests including a bilingual evaluator's failed effort to engage my son in a basic conversation, a speech-language pathologist concluded that our family should focus on one language only to avoid any further confusions or delays. As it turned out, a partial hearing loss due to a severe ear infection in one ear, not his bilingualism, caused my son's challenges. So, my advice? Let's all bust myths and challenge misconceptions!

Possible sources of biases and mistaken beliefs regarding bi- or multilingualism may be linked to a number of historical or outdated scientific claims, negative attitudes toward immigration, language suppression whereby immigrant parents stopped speaking their primary language to their children, and the detrimental impact of the "English only" movement, just to name a few. Other myths are perpetuated by a limited understanding of or access to the latest research in the field of neurolinguistics and cognitive science. In fact, bilingualism and multilingualism have been empirically linked to several cognitive advantages, including heightened cross-cultural awareness and communicative sensitivity, more advanced executive function skills, and divergent thinking, perspective taking, and problem-solving skills, while research continues to strengthen these claims (Kroll & Dussias, 2017; Poarch & Krott, 2019). As educators, we, too, must commit to continued shared learning about our students' multilingual experiences, as well as keep up with ongoing and emerging research from the field.

Tapestry of Voices

Kathy Escamilla, professor of education in the Division of Social, Bilingual and Multicultural Foundations at the University of Colorado, cautions against persistent harmful practices such as these:

> *English only assessment practices, especially high stakes testing; English only instructional materials, direct translations of English only instructional materials and assessments into other languages, misunderstanding of bilingual behaviors (e.g. translanguaging) as deficits.*

Luciana C. de Oliveira, Professor, Department of Teaching and Learning, School of Education, Virginia Commonwealth University, Richmond, VA, also calls attention to prevailing English-only practices and cautions against the following:

> *Pedagogy that is not inclusive of multilingual students' backgrounds and experiences; giving students different opportunities (ex: having them doing simple tasks and others more complex tasks); and simplifying tasks and texts for multilingual students.*

Notable Research

Barbara Hofer synthesized important developments in research on multilingualism and multi-competence and reviewed findings from empirical studies into early multilingual competence. Her aim was to "promote a balanced and research-based discussion of multilingual competence, advance understanding of how being multilingual affects young children's language development and cognition and rectify monolingual-biased axioms about purportedly debilitating consequences of multilingualism" (Hofer, 2025, p. 548).

Linguistic Family History or Autobiography

I invite you to engage in a brief, informal autoethnographic research about your own or your family's experiences with languages to enhance your self-awareness of what languages and your linguistic heritage mean to you. Anne H. Charity Hudley and Nelson Flores remind us that "anybody who studies issues of language is a linguist" (2022, p. 146), so don't hesitate to think about and explore some personally meaningful aspects of language and language learning. Yolanda Sealey-Ruiz (2026) recently published a fascinating book in the Equity and Social Justice in Education Series, called *Archaeology of Self: The Introspective Educator's Guide to Racial Literacy*, in which she invites her readers to uncover the heart of teaching by engaging in the critical work of self-discovery. Inspired by her work, I, too, engage both pre-service and in-service educators in their linguistic exploration.

Tapestry of Voices

Among several other recommendations, Joanna Kolota, Curriculum Leader: Multilingual Learners at Trinity Academy Leeds, UK also emphasizes the need for on-going equity-centered learning, critical self-reflection, and deeply reflective identity work:

> *The ability to recognize even the subtlest biases and inequities represents the greatest urgency in our schools today. Without this foundational skill, it becomes nearly impossible to respond, redress, or sustain equity efforts. Recognition is the first step toward meaningful action; if we cannot identify bias or inequity, we cannot challenge or change it.*
>
> *Teachers and students could engage in structured reflection about their own identities, cultural lenses. By better understanding how our backgrounds influence our perceptions, we become more attuned to recognising subtle forms of bias and inequity in our schools.*
>
> *Staff and students also need sustained, reflective training/assemblies/lessons that go beyond surface-level diversity workshops. For teachers this could include learning on how implicit biases show up in curriculum, classroom management, expectations for students and language use, especially for multilingual learners.*

You might be wondering if I am going to assign you a research project or expect you to write a paper and might be ready to close the book or skip the rest of this section but hear me out! This type of self-discovery might give you just the opportunity you need to reflect on the many factors that have influenced your language(s) and how the language(s) in your life or your family's lives have influenced you. In other words, I am inviting you to tell your linguistic story! Tell it to the smallest audience (just you) or the largest crowd (turn it into a TED Talk) you wish to share it with but consider the power of uncovering what mattered in the past about languages and what continues to matter to you now and in the future.

Think about, talk about, ask family members about, journal about, sketch, draw, or write about the role of language(s) in your life and the relationship of language to your identity development. You may also reflect on how a variety of languages and/or dialects have been used, retained or lost over the decades in your family. If you wish to go deeper into your family history, you can consider how language policies have impacted your own family's private decisions about languages. And if you are not sure where to start, just begin by jotting down some ideas in response to these questions, interview your elders in the family, engage in a conversation with someone in your household, or find a distant cousin who is also interested in languages.

Some possible questions to get you started:

- What languages and/or dialects do you speak? How about your immediate and extended family?
- How does your language reflect your upbringing?
- What has influenced the way you use language every day? How about in professional settings?
- When, if ever, do you alter your speech and why?
- What kind of differences do you notice between the way you speak and write?

Are you up for some more questions to guide your reflection?

- Do you have childhood memories that revolve around language(s)?
- How and when is language used in your family?
- In what ways do you see your language as part of your identity?
- What sort of language was spoken in your neighborhood where you grew up? How about where you live now?
- What other languages have you studied?

- What linguistics adventures or mishaps have you had if any?
- What other languages have you used for communication?
- What languages or dialects did your parents or grandparents speak?
- Do any members of your extended family come from a unique language background?
- What languages have or haven't been spoken across generations?
- Are there any names, phrases, stories or songs passed down in your family that preserved your linguistic heritage?
- What are your family's attitudes about language?

For inspiration, see this reflection from a Regional Bilingual Education Network administrator (all names are retained at the request of the author to celebrate the rich linguistic family history represented in the essay). Such deep reflection not only holds up a generational and historical mirror, but it also builds empathy and understanding for others.

A Linguistic Journey Through My Family

My maternal grandmother, Isabel Adorno, was born and raised in Puerto Rico. Her formal education was sporadic and did not extend beyond the sixth grade level, so although she was a native Spanish speaker, she spoke primarily in dialect and slang customary to her family and region. To another Spanish speaker, the level of grammar and lexicon evident in her speech would be clear indicators of her socio-economic background, as well as her education level. Isabel came to America as a teenager in the early 1900s and was exposed for the first time to the English language. By the age of 18, she had met and married my maternal grandfather, Julio Fairchild.

Julio was born and raised in the Philippines, to a Philippine mother and an English father. His first language was Tagalog, but he was formally educated in English, starting in early childhood through the high school level, and was proficient in this second language. Through his studies, he was also exposed to a lesser extent to the Spanish language and acquired an intermediate proficiency. He came to America in his early 20s, and joined the American Navy, giving him the opportunity to further hone his English skills. He married my grandmother at the age of 28.

My grandparents had obvious language barriers between them. However, they were able to communicate primarily in Spanish, in which Julio acquired a greater proficiency over the course of their marriage. His success in learning Spanish through conversation and necessity may be attributed to the following observation: "Acquisition requires meaningful interaction in the target language—natural communication—in which speakers are concerned not with the form of their utterances but with the messages they are conveying and understanding" (Krashen, n.d.). At the same time, my grandmother was gaining additional exposure to English.

Together Isabel and Julio had five children before Julio died at the age of 45. The first three children, Henry, Louis and Gladys, were close in age, and spoke informal Spanish in the home with my grandparents. They never learned Tagalog but would often hear my grandfather speaking this language with his friends. They also used English with my grandfather, as well as outside the home and in their neighborhood. This was a common practice at the time among children of immigrant parents; speaking English outside the home helped them to socially assimilate in their vastly diverse community.

Once they began school, they quickly increased their fluency as English speakers. This was critical to their achievement in school, where all general instruction was conducted in English. By the time their two younger siblings, Alice and Norma, were born, the primary language the children spoke in the house was English, although my grandmother continued to speak to them only in Spanish. For this reason, Alice and Norma, who fully understood Spanish, were not fluent speakers in this language while growing up but did acquire speaking fluency after studying formal Spanish in high school and college. To this day, the five siblings notice a difference between the informal dialect learned and used by the three older children, and the more academic version of Spanish used by the two youngest. For Gladys and Louis in particular, who never studied formal Spanish, these differences often resulted in embarrassment over not using the "correct" Spanish and made them hesitant to use it in public situations.

Meanwhile, in another section of Brooklyn, my paternal grandmother, Mary Matika, was a first-generation English-speaking American, from a Hungarian family. She married Donald Alger, also an English speaker. They raised three children, Don, Arthur and Mary, whose accents reveal their Brooklyn upbringing. In their early childhood, they heard Hungarian being spoken between their mother and grandmother. None of the children acquired this language, and upon their grandmother's death, Hungarian was no longer used in their household.

My parents are Norma Fairchild and Don Alger. They raised my two sisters and me in Queens, where my mother worked, and continues to work to spare us from succumbing to a Queens accent; continuously correcting our diction, grammar, and pronunciation. She has had varied success over the years, and has now focused her attention on "saving" her grandchildren.

Growing up, my maternal grandmother was an influential presence in my life. I have distinct memories of Spanish children's songs she would teach us ("ventana—window, puerta—door, lápiz—pencil, y piso—floor"), her greetings and goodbyes in Spanish (¡Hola, mi hija! = hello, my child; dame un beso = give me a kiss), and her commands at the dinner table (¡sientate! = sit!, ¡come! = eat!). She spoke "broken" English, or "Spanglish," to her grandchildren, with a heavy Spanish accent, and we would hear her speaking Spanish with our mother, aunts and uncles. Another phrase often entwined in her speech was, "¿Cómo se dice ...?, " or, "How do you say ...?" She struggled constantly to speak to us in English and did increase her proficiency through the years by working at various factories and jobs.

As a child, I was often embarrassed if my grandmother spoke Spanish in front of my friends; this made me different, when all I wanted was to fit in with everyone else. Looking back as an adult, I wish that my grandmother and my mother would have made more of an effort to immerse me in Spanish while I was growing up, so that I would have been naturally bilingual, rather than attempting to acquire it as a second language later in life. Although I did study Spanish for several years in middle and high schools, as well as college, I never considered myself fluent and continue to be hesitant to speak Spanish with my relatives. I believe that my ability to acquire a second language at that later age had diminished from what it may have been in my early childhood.

While I have no cognizance of my own language acquisition in English, I am now continually amazed as I watch my young children progress from the babbling of their pre-linguistic stages to the utterance of their first words and then sentences. My children are currently studying Spanish in school and are receiving reinforcement at home through their grandmother and great aunt. I hope to recover and preserve this element of our linguistic and cultural identities.

Pause for a Moment

What stood out to you from the example above?

What similarities and differences do you see in this story compared to yours?

What would you highlight in your linguistic autobiography or family history?

Listening with Intent

Listening to multilingual learners and other multilingual members of the school community can and will be eye- (or ear-) opening! What are their stories? What do they experience? What are their truths that needs to be told, heard, and retold?

As a language educator, I came across a fascinating poem, "Listening with TING," by Sally Huang-Nissen (1999) in her book about engaging in cross-cultural dialogue. The Chinese character for listening illustrates how complex and comprehensive it truly is to listen because it involves six distinct elements all brought together (see Figure 2.1).

Ears to hear the words
Eyes to see the person and watch for body language
Mind to understand and process what is being said
King/Respect to treat the speaker like royalty, with utmost respect
Oneness to give one's full attention and to focus on the speaker
Heart to feel and be compassionate

Unpacking what it means to listen with *ting* turned into a regular feature of my professional learning sessions, giving participating educators a much-needed opportunity to reflect on whether we truly listen to each other, especially when there are (perceived) cultural and linguistic barriers to consider or biases and misconceptions to uncover or courageously face. Deconstructing

Figure 2.1 The Chinese character of *ting* (listen).

Table 2.1 Core skills of radical listening applied to multilingual conversations.

Types of listening skills	Six core skills	Brief definitions	Applications to listening to multilingual members of the school community
Internal	Noticing	Being fully present	Look at the person you are talking to, not the interpreter (if there is one) Understand different cultural norms for body language (including eye contact)
	Quieting	Avoiding distractions	Find a quiet place that removes noise and distractions from the conversation Show patience and allow extra time for processing and responding
	Accepting	Respecting differences	Anticipate unique perspectives and cultural knowledge to be shared Accept cultural differences in conversation styles and norms
External	Acknowledging	Validating others	Focus on the strengths and assets (not deficiencies or problems) that are brought into the conversation
	Questioning	Showing sincere interest	Ask for more information that reveals genuine curiosity about the student/family without prying Acknowledge what you do not know and take the opportunity to learn about the student's language, family and culture
	Interjecting	Engaging without interrupting	Limit verbal interjections (they might interrupt the speakers' train of thought), choose nonverbal signals to show you are listening and encouraging the speaker to continue Avoid offering quick solutions to complex issues or hijacking the conversation

and reconstructing the Chinese character of *ting* and applying the process to the kinds of listening we need to engage in personally and professionally leads to deep moments of reflection.

Let's fast forward a few (thousand) years and find Christian van Nieuwerburgh and Robert Biswas-Diener (2025) reminding us to consider a new approach to listening. In their book *Radical Listening*, they argue that listening is not made radical by something outrageous or shocking, instead, it is connected to two core beliefs consisting of three internal and three external listening skills. Internal listening focuses on the way we pay attention and remain quiet and focused and external skills refer to how we actively engage during listening. The applicability of this framework to understanding the multilingual experience is profound.

With radical listening, we set clear intentions and aim to go beyond comprehension: "listening is one of the most effective ways of strengthening relationships and creating opportunities. It replaces the concept of 'information' with that of 'connection'" (van Nieuwerburgh & Robert Biswas-Diener, 2025, p. 6). The six radical listening skills are divided into internal and external ones, which are briefly summarized in Table 2.1. Considering conversations with multilingual members of the school community (students and family members), I connect the six core skills to the theme of this book in the final column of the chart. These applications highlight unique opportunities to further enhance listening skills when multilingual members of the community are involved and learning about one's own misconceptions and biases through the process.

Pause for a Moment

What aspects of listening with *ting* or radical listening have you found most affirming or most challenging when it comes to interactions with multilingual members of your school community?

Why is listening to others important when considering multilingual inequities or injustices?

How can you apply one or both of these frameworks to listening to your colleagues, including fellow educators, administrators, staff members, or school board officials?

Committing to Deeper Work

After engaging in some crucial but sometimes personally challenging internal work of examining your own biases, prejudices, or misconceptions, we now move into intentionally looking for language-based inequities or injustices connected to multilingualism in your immediate school context.

BIASES
PREJUDICES
DISCRIMINATION
DISPARITIES
INEQUITIES
INJUSTICES

Surveys for Educators

What would members of your school community have to say when presented with three simple sentence starters at the next faculty meeting?

Multilingual learners are …

Multilingual learners can …

Multilingual learners will …

What descriptive words or phrases would they use to complete the first sentence? What abilities would they highlight for the second sentence stem? How would they envision the future for this population when finishing the third sentence? A survey, a focus group discussion, or even responses to a simple, anonymous digital tool such as Answergarden (www.answergraden.ch) or Mentimeter (www.menti.com) could yield important insights into the general consensus among the faculty while also shedding light on some less commonly held, or even isolated, but damaging or detrimental opinions that might be shared. Based on the data gathered formally or informally, with or without names, in writing or through courageous, difficult conversation, further equity-oriented discussions could take place to better understand the following:

- What are some powerful examples of uplifting, identity-affirming, and linguistically responsive and sustaining stories of multilingualism or multilingual students and families? Where do they come from?
- Are there any examples of savior mentality (the desire to over cuddle and rescue multilingual learners) included and what or where do such inclinations stem from?
- What experiences or perceptions are potential sources of negative views, biases, prejudices, overgeneralizations? Where do deficit-based ideologies come from?

The goal is to clearly see, hear, and bravely name inequities and injustices and to engage in deeper dialogues in a safe professional environment. One conversation is not sufficient! In the next chapter, we will return to naming negative perceptions and changing the narrative about multilingualism by showcasing authentic stories of challenges multilingual learners overcame and opportunities they embraced to succeed.

Tapestry of Voices

Montserrat Garibay, former Deputy Secretary of the U.S. Department of Education and Director of the Office of English Language Acquisition, shares several additional suggestions for self-reflection and initiating critical conversations, such as the following:

> *Encourage self-reflection and awareness by sharing ways to check our implicit bias, offer trainings to acknowledge and address bias and inequalities, create systems to reduce it, find ways to question status quo, seek out and engage with marginalized communities, focus on the root causes of inequality and have courageous conversations.*

Shadowing

As the old adage says, seeing is believing! So far, I encouraged you to do a lot of listening, keep an ear to the ground, and understand what people are saying, thinking, and believing (even if you do not necessarily agree with them). But what if we could more closely examine the day-to-day realities of multilingual learners? There is a protocol for it frequently referred to as shadowing developed by Ivannia Soto (2021) and further adapted by the New York State Department of Education (n.d.).

To get started, when you shadow a student, you follow them from class to class for an entire day and observe their academic and linguistic experiences. Using a multilingual lens, I invite you to try the observation tool in Figure 2.2 and document how frequently and when the student has the opportunity to use one or more of their languages and literacies. Based on the WIDA (2020) frameworks, the core modes of communication (interpretive, expressive, and interactive) are augmented to include supports; those that are visually accessing (viewing, watching, closely examining visual input such as pictures, photographs, artwork, charts, graphs, videos, etc.) and visually representing (drawing, sketching, illustrating, depicting, completing a graphic organizer, etc.) concepts. The tool invites you to add the languages the student uses and to include additional anecdotal notes and details at the bottom of the template. If there are more than two languages involved, simply add one more column to the right. Finally, feel free to adapt the tool as you see fit.

One of my first shadowing experiences that I conducted in a middle school allowed me to follow a small group of students from class to class all day long. I sat in the back of the room and not surprisingly, the three students who I was observing also sat in the back in all but one of the 7 class periods.

Table 2.2 Language-focused shadowing protocol.

Primary communicative focus	**Communicative domains**	**Language 1: __________**	**Language 2: __________**
Interpretive	Listening		
	Reading		
	Visually accessing		
Expressive	Speaking		
	Writing		
	Visually representing		
Additional notes			
Goals for next shadowing:			

The shadowing data so painfully revealed that some students went through an entire day either quietly sitting, looking, and feeling left out and checked out or chatting in their home language while being off task and not engaged academically. What are the dangers of marginalizing students because of perceived language barriers?

Missed Opportunities

Contributions are missed
Insights are ignored
Opportunity to shine is squandered
Sense of belonging is diminished
Silence speaking louder than any words in any language might!

A single day or even a single period of shadowing can be informative. However, as an on-going, joint professional learning project, I developed a five-part shadowing protocol inspired by Ivannia Soto's (2021) work that may be used over several days or weeks and lead to deep, collaborative explorations of how multilingual learners are engaged in learning (see textbox).

Multi-Part Shadowing Protocol

- ★ ***Task 1: Shadowing***
  a. Familiarize yourself with the shadowing protocol based on Ivannia Soto's work
  b. Use key elements of the protocol as you closely observe the student
  c. Collect evidence of student language use (including observation data and student work samples and artifacts) over several days or weeks
  d. Describe the student's language and literacy development stage
  e. Determine the student's areas of strengths and needs
- ★ ***Task 2: Planning***
  a. Based on the shadowing experience and data, identify key long-term learning goals for the student
  b. Plan a lesson sequence with immediate language- and literacy-based learning targets
  c. Include specific strategies that respond to the student's developmental needs while highlighting their strengths
  d. Justify your instruction with a brief explanation of key theory and research relevant to multilingual education
- ★ ***Task 3: Instruction***
  a. Implement your plan with careful consideration of the shadowing data
  b. Engage your student in language-based tasks that align with their needs while highlighting their strengths
  c. Continue monitoring the student's progress

★ ***Task 4: Assessment and reflection***

a. Provide feedback and guidance to your student based on their strengths and needs
b. Analyze your student's development over the course of the project using specific evidence from work samples and observations
c. Reflect on the student's progress and anticipate future needs

★ ***Task 5: Reporting***

a. Keep a journal of your activities and your student's responses, work samples, and progress
b. In your journal, reflect on your planning, instruction, and assessment according to the outline above
c. Analyze what the student experienced as a language learner during this shadowing project
d. Prepare a brief, a cohesive report at the end of the 2- to 4-week shadowing experience discussing what worked, what did not work, (and why) as well as how the student responded to instruction during the shadowing experience

Tapestry of Voices

Shadia Salem, Assistant Superintendent of English Learning, North Palos School District 117, Illinois, offers some of her recommendations to develop the first equity literacy ability, while also acknowledging the importance of shadowing students:

> *The ability to recognize even the subtlest biases and inequities is crucial. Some approaches can include first training on recognizing it—by self-reflecting or doing tabletop activities of situations. Another idea can be to shadow students and teachers, do walkthroughs based off of a survey so when collecting data, you can recognize this is an issue. You can also do cultural competency training, and you can audit your current practices against a rubric. It is also important to hold people accountable and have critical conversations about the findings.*

Stacy Brown, English Language Learner (ELL) Compliance Coordinator with the Oklahoma City Public Schools, Oklahoma, highlights the importance of inclusivity to get a more complete picture of inequities and injustices:

> *In order to recognize even the subtlest biases and inequities, we must start with inclusive practices that not just allow but require equitable input on the development and employment of all approaches.*

> *The processes for reviewing materials, policies, and practices must be actively equitable and ongoing. Some districts might have an advisory committee enabling parents and guardians to inform schools and districts, but participation is limited by timing, requiring in-person meetings, and other common restrictions. Approaches should include actively engaging all participants in self-reflection and inviting participant feedback and criticism in ways that fully empower them to take part, regardless of their role or background. Districts, schools, and educators often employ online surveys but intentionally and unintentionally limit input to participants who have access to WIFI, speak, read, and write certain languages, and use email and other forms of technology. Approaches must empower equal participation regardless of literacy levels, technology availability, the ability to see or hear, etc. Additionally, all participants should be afforded the privilege to refine and deepen their ability to reflect, observe, analyze, and recognize inequities and biases, being given the same quality of opportunities and "training" as all involved professionals.*

Multilingual Equity Talks

Before engaging in a more formal inquiry, here is another powerful challenge to try. Start with one conversation. Sit down with just one colleague, a coach, or a small group of educators and talk about your students. Guide the conversation to be about one or more multilingual learners; share what you notice about them, ask what others are concerned about, and end by affirming why it is so important to talk about the unique experiences of multilingual learners. The conversation might stop right there, and it might have to be picked up at a later time. When you do continue, consider some more pointed questions to guide your equity talk:

- In what ways are multilingual learners included or excluded from academic and nonacademic opportunities?
- What manifestations of language-based discriminations can be detected?
- How much of their linguistic repertoires and rich multilingual heritages are the students using in school?

You might wish to expand the multilingual equity talks to explore a particular curricular area, a recent or outdated district policy, a school tradition or any other aspect of school life that may impact multilingual learners in a negative way.

Multilingual Equity Walks

Whether the multilingual equity talk results in a little or a lot in terms of multilingual inequities, the more the reason to take a more careful look in the form of a multilingual equity walk. When I suggest you take a walk, you may do so alone or with one or more colleagues. Consider it to take the form of both a physical walk and a virtual one:

- The first type of walk will take you throughout the entire school building. The goal is to notice and note any evidence of possible inequities or biases that you might witness in classrooms and other physical spaces. Repeated walks are likely to uncover a more nuanced perspective on multilingual learners' experiences.
- A second, virtual walk might take you in a different direction. I am suggesting looking through documents such as written policies, curriculum guides, email and other types of communication to care givers and so on and start noticing examples of possible sources of inequities.

As I am finishing this chapter with these last two recommendations (multilingual equity talks and multilingual equity walks), the play on words is too tempting to skip. Let's agree to talk the talk and walk the walk, when it comes to multilingual justice!

Spotlight on Multilingual Justice

Andrea Bitner, Author, PD Partner, and EL Educator at Interboro School District, Prospect Park, Pennsylvania, shares a story that underscores why recognizing inequities and advocating for justice for multilingual learners is critical:

> In late winter, when course recommendation forms begin circulating and eighth graders start talking about high school like it's a country just over the horizon, Denver came into my classroom practically glowing.

"It's recommendation time," he said, dropping into his seat but unable to sit still. "I'm getting ready for high school."

There was something electric in his voice—not nervousness, not doubt. Anticipation.

Denver is one of our English learners, still acquiring the language, still reaching for vocabulary that doesn't always come easily. But if you watched him in class—really watched him—you wouldn't see hesitation. You'd see a student who is doing the work.

He completes assignments on time.

He revises without complaint.

He raises his hand—sometimes searching for the exact word, sometimes stitching together a sentence in real time—but always willing to try.

His grades reflect that effort. They aren't inflated. They aren't the result of lowered expectations. They are earned. Steady A's and strong B's in core classes. Growth across the board. Teacher comments about persistence, curiosity, and leadership in group work.

Denver knows this. He tracks his progress carefully. So when he told me he wanted to sign up for higher-level classes in high school, it wasn't a whim. It was a plan.

"I want to take honors English," he said. "And maybe advanced science. I think I can do it."

He wasn't asking for a favor. He was asking for access.

But when he met with some of his middle school teachers, the response was more cautious.

They weren't unkind. They weren't dismissive. They were "concerned."

High school is harder.

The texts are more complex.

The writing expectations increase.

And, well ... he's still an English learner.

The hesitation lingered in the air, even if no one meant harm by it.

What if it's too much?

What if the language load is overwhelming?

What if he struggles?

But here's the question that echoed louder for me: What if he thrives?

Denver has already shown us who he is.

He is the student who comes in during lunch to clarify feedback.

He is the student who rewrites an introduction three times because he wants it to be stronger.

He is the student who volunteers to read aloud—accent and all—because he refuses to let language insecurity silence him.

Language acquisition is a process. It is not a measure of intelligence. It is not a ceiling on potential. And it is certainly not a reason to deny opportunity when a student is demonstrating readiness.

Holding Denver back because his English isn't perfect would be like benching a player who's scoring—just because he's still learning the playbook.

He is scoring.

His grades prove it.

His work ethic proves it.

His confidence—that bright, anticipatory confidence when he walked in talking about high school—proves it.

When we withhold advanced placement from students like Denver, we tell them, quietly, that effort isn't enough. That achievement isn't enough. That growth isn't enough. We mistake accent for ability. We confuse language development with limitation.

And yet, Denver is already climbing.

He's climbing every time he participates.

Every time he revises.

Every time he chooses the harder path instead of the easier one.

Course recommendation season is about predicting success. But sometimes the evidence is right in front of us. Sometimes the safest choice isn't the most protective one—it's the one that trusts the student who has already shown us he can rise.

Moving Beyond Recognizing Multilingual Inequities

Recognizing multilingual inequities and injustices is a necessary first step in naming abilities that constitute the equity literacy framework, but we cannot stop here. Listening tours, self-reflections, shadowing protocols, and multilingual equity walks will all support an honest look at what is happening to our multilingual learners inside and out of school. How are we going to respond to the inequities we uncover? What are we going do to once we cannot unsee the injustices? The next two chapters will uncover short-term and long-term next steps to respond to and redress inequities!

End-of-Chapter Reflections

As you finish exploring the first ability of equity literacy, to recognize inequities and injustices, reflect on the following:

- Why is it vital to be able to recognize, name, and intentionally look for evidence of multilingual inequities or injustices in our schools?
- What types of deficit-oriented perspectives have you encountered in your own context?
- How do the examples compare to your own experiences?
- Which practical strategies are most appealing to you?

3

How to Respond to Multilingual Inequities and Injustices

A Promise

A promise to listen
A promise to understand
A promise to speak up
A promise to call in
A promise to learn
A promise to dialogue
A promise to act

I have always been fascinated by historical linguistics. Where do languages and words come from? How did words and concepts pass from culture to culture, from language to language over time? What could have shaped the meaning of words as they traveled across time? So, allow me to indulge in a little linguistic exploration. The origin of the English word *respond* has some insightful connotations I can't help but share with you. The Latin root *re-* means "again" and *spondore* means to promise or to pledge. Historically, *respond* means to promise again, to pledge again. Let's hold on to that original meaning of the word for a bit and reflect on the power of first recognizing multilingual inequities and injustices (as we did in Chapter 2) and then respond to such inequities. What is our response going to be? What is our promise? What is our pledge to multilingual students and their families?

DOI: 10.4324/9781003644071-3

In this chapter, we are focusing on how to respond in the moment, in the immediate term, whereas our promise or pledge will continue in Chapter 4, where we explore how to redress or respond with longer-term actions at the institutional or deeper level. As you will see, we have a lot of opportunities to make a commitment, a promise, a pledge, and then to act on those promises!

Which of these have you heard? From students:

- *I can't do this.*
- *It is too hard.*
- *No speak English.*
- *Nobody knows what I am thinking or feeling!*
- *I wish my teachers knew how smart I am, but my ideas don't seem to come out right in English!*
- *I am so scared to speak, I don't want anybody to laugh at me.*
- *I don't think they [teachers] care about us!*

From families:

- *We don't understand.*
- *They [educators] don't understand what we have been through.*
- *We don't know how to help our children.*
- *They [educators] don't know how to help our children.*

From colleagues:

- *I can't teach math if they don't speak English.*
- *I wish they practiced English at home.*
- *Those kids need to learn proper English/good English/appropriate English.*
- *The parents don't really care about their kids' education, they never show up to any school events, they did not even come to parent-teacher conferences even though I sent home the note translated into their language.*
- *They just want to speak in* _______ [fill in a language other than English] *in my class and I don't even know what they are talking about, but I am sure it is not history.*

Pause for a Moment

What do you say when you hear any of these? How do those conversations typically go?

What have you tried to do in response to any similar sentiments or claims? Who are your allies to plan some actionable next steps?

Deficit Ideologies

At the core of all of these and many other similar sentiments is deficit-oriented thinking. Deficit ideologies, biases, and prejudices are not reserved for multilingual learners! Sadly, they seem to permeate the field of education and impact all marginalized and minoritized communities. Paul Gorski and Katy Swalwell (2023a) argue that deficit ideologies lead to wrongfully blaming minoritized groups' educational disparities on their "moral, intellectual, dispositional, or even spiritual deficiencies" (p. 97) instead of recognizing the complex conditions, societal and institutional inequities they experience. According to deficit-oriented approaches, we need to fix what is wrong (with the students) or what is inadequate (about them), and all the problems or disparities will disappear, right? Not so fast! Inspired by Gorski and Swalwell's work, I, too, challenge you to confront deficit ideologies and recognize that structural inequities cannot be resolved though deficit-thinking because such ideologies simply mask or further obscure the real challenges!

Language-based deficit ideologies have prevailed despite expanding research that recognizes the strengths and assets multilingualism and multilingual learners represent. They unfortunately turned into mental models that seem to inform instructional practices. I created a summary chart in Table 3.1 to highlight some key examples of deficit-based orientation to multilingualism and multilingual learners and what rejecting such ideologies might look like. I added ample space at the bottom of the chart for you to continue adding examples for both from your context and to reflect on the mental models that permeate your educational context.

We also know that it is never only about language. Oppressive or deficit-oriented beliefs about languages or multilingualism "are always intertwined with ideologies of culture, nationality, race, ethnicity, gender, sexuality, and ableism, amongst others" and are connected to "how we understand the nature, acquisition, and use of language" (Yazan, 2025, p. xii).

- What do we know or believe to be true about first and subsequent language acquisition?
- What do we know or believe to be true about the rich variety of languages and dialects that exist in our classrooms, schools, and communities?
- What do we know or believe about the hierarchical positions associated with languages?
- Why are certain language users and language learners privileged in schools and society?
- Whose languages are valued? Who is admired as a polyglot?
- Who is only noticed for their emerging English skills?

Table 3.1 Assuming and rejecting deficit-based orientations to multilingualism and multilingual learners.

When educators have a deficit-based orientation to multilingualism and multilingual learners, they believe and act upon the following:	When educators reject a deficit-based approach to multilingualism and multilingual learners, they believe and act upon the following:
Learning standard English is of utmost priority and the only way to academic success	Developing multilingual capacity is valued and a clear path is created to achieving it
Focusing on what the students do not have or cannot do	Focusing on what the students have or can do
Identifying achievement gaps and connecting them to students' proficiency in English	Identifying opportunity gaps and connecting them to systemic or structural inequities
Seeing language learners as deficient or inferior who cannot achieve academically	Seeing multilingual language learners as linguistically gifted
Suggesting that multilingual learners cannot learn rigorous academic content without developing fluency in academic English first	Recognizing multimodal and multilingual opportunities for rigorous academic learning
Blaming the students or their families or linguistic/ cultural groups for disparities in educational outcomes	Focusing on educational systems or societal factors instead of blaming individuals

Several decades ago, Ricardo Ruíz (1984) presented a tri-part language-planning framework capturing society's and educators' basic orientations towards languages. The fundamental question was whether we see language as a problem, a right, or a resource. Ruíz's work continues to be highly influential not only for understanding how language planning policies emerged but also how deficit-oriented perspectives were reinforced by policies. His framework serves as a helpful springboard to shift the conversation about multilingualism, to understand the complexity of language planning, and to take action around these orientations.

If you are new to Ricardo Ruíz's work, or need a quick refresher, here is a brief overview:

- ***When language is viewed as a problem,*** linguistic diversity and languages are tied to social problems, so eradicating nondominant languages will contribute to solving those social ills. Monolingualism is the norm, with the dominant language (standard English) viewed as superior to all other languages or varieties of Englishes. Linguistic diversity may even be perceived as a threat to national unity, so all nondominant language speakers are expected to assimilate to achieve social cohesion. Learning English is also believed to help provide opportunities to everyone.
- ***When language is viewed as a right,*** individuals and communities reject the language-as-a-problem perspective and demand legal guarantees to be put in place. When language rights are recognized as a civil right or human right issue, speakers of nondominant languages receive protections to hold on to their heritages and cultural identities as well as have access to education and other public services without discrimination!
- ***When language is viewed as a resource,*** linguistic diversity no longer poses a threat; just the opposite, it is considered a valuable asset for both individuals speaking languages other than English and for society as a whole. Ricardo Ruíz advocated for this third orientation to help bridge the gap between the first two (language as a problem and language as a right) as well as to recognize and preserve all languages for the benefit of humankind.

While I was working on this manuscript, the Office of the Attorney General (2025) published a memo, indicating a return to the most restricting, language-as-a-problem policy orientation, rescinding prior guidance regarding LEP (Limited English Proficient) persons, naming one of goals as assimilation.

Further changes to policy regarding language access and multilingualism can be anticipated:

> *The Department will complete a full internal inventory of all existing non-English services, and release Department-wide plans to phase out unnecessary multilingual offerings. The Department will consider redirecting these funds towards research and programs that would expedite English-language acquisition and increase English-language proficiency and assimilation.*
>
> (Office of the Attorney General, 2025, p. 2)

During volatile political times, continued equity work for multilingualism, multilingual learners, and immigrant-origin youths and families is more critical than ever before. Advocacy on behalf of vulnerable student populations such as undocumented students' right to a free and appropriate education must continue!

Sometimes, attitudes toward languages may show up in an educational context as more than just a one-dimensional, clear-cut orientation: it may be viewed as a problem and resource, or as a resource and a right, or perhaps even at the intersection of all three. Educators' daily practices, their own lived experiences, and school policies may not align: an ELA (English Language Arts) educator who happens to be bilingual may engage in translanguaging pedagogy with a newcomer student in a school that has an English-only language support program. What is happening here? The teacher recognizes her and her students' right to use their shared heritage language, which also serves as a resource for the student to have access to the ELA curriculum. At the same time, there is no bilingual program option available, so the de facto language policy is to learn English and to learn in English.

Pause for a Moment

In what way(s) has Ruíz's tri-part framework affirmed or challenged your prior knowledge of viewing languages and language policies in different ways?

Do educators typically see language as a problem, a right, or a resource in schools and classrooms?

How do these educational orientations manifest themselves in your context?

What short-term steps might you take to alleviate or mitigate the prevailing view of language?

Let's take it a step further and ask the same question a bit differently. What might this three-part framework mean for multilingualism and multilingual learners when looking through an equity lens within educational settings? How can inherent, blatant or less perceptible, hidden inequities can be addressed by taking a closer look at multilingualism this way ...

When multilingualism is viewed as a problem:

- There might be explicitly written district or school policies about the use of English for educational or communication purposes
- Monolingualism remains the norm in the curricular, instructional, and assessment resources and practices
- English is declared as the ultimate goal and a pathway to academic participation and success
- Teachers feel insecure about having multilingual learners in their classrooms due to a number of possible factors:
    - a lack of or limited preservice and in-service preparation for working with multilingual learners
    - a lack of or limited experience teaching students who come from or with a range of language backgrounds
    - a lack of or limited knowledge of languages
    - fear of failure and embarrassment about inadequacy as an educator
- Students are prevented from or punished for using any language other than English
- Students see their own multilingualism as a problem, a source of shame or avoidance

Becki Cohn-Vargas and Debbie Zacarian (2024) caution that "for many multilingual learners, being limited from speaking their own language is a form of cultural erasure that can lead to rejection of their home language" (p. 8). Jim Cummins's (2001) similar, frequently cited message continues to ring true, "To reject a child's language in the school is to reject the child" (p. 19). Whether rejection happens externally or internally, through explicit federal, state, or district policy or intentional gatekeeping, multilingual learners feel it, internalize it, and may become less engaged and less socially or academically present.

Educators hold the power to invent and enact everyday language policies, be it whether they allow any primary or home language use in the classroom, if translated materials will be made available, if students can use an app on their phone, if they establish bilingual peer bridges, if they engage in translanguaging and so on. I have witnessed it firsthand, so come back in time with me to an early December afternoon.

We are visiting a middle school, a very special place where I happily joined the faculty multiple times to offer sustained professional development on best practices for multilingual learners. At the end of another successful half-day of joint learning (you do what you can, right?), I merrily walked down the hallway already thinking of my next visit, eagerly planning how we can further the work. As I was leaving the building, suddenly, I heard a loud call.

"English, please!"

My heart jumped! I turned around, thinking for a moment the voice was calling after me! I saw a teacher confronting two boys who were chatting and laughing about something in Spanish as they were hurrying to their next class or perhaps to lunch! To my relief, it was not one of the teachers with whom I have worked over several months. I did not know this teacher but felt obliged to say hello and engage in a however short conversation we might have about what I just witnessed. I had no intention of turning this unforeseen encounter with a teacher I never met into an on-the-spot confrontation or a lecture, and I definitely did not plan to continue my professional learning session in the hallway, uninvited, but I had to do something. I could not simply ask, "Why did you just say that!?" Rather than feeling frustrated, mostly, I was driven by curiosity.

Why was this teacher so bothered by two students talking in the hallway during the three-minute break they have between classes in their shared home language? What was so offensive, disturbing, or upsetting to her that she needed to publicly call out the students?

I stepped to the side to allow the teacher to catch up to me since she was heading my way! I said a friendly hello and quickly introduced myself. She knew about the workshops I was offering but did not seem to make a connection between why I was in the school and what I would want to talk to her about. After a moment of pause, I simply stated what a productive day I had with her colleagues and shared with her what a welcoming experience I have had all these months coming to the school. I asked if she taught the two boys who just passed us and when she said yes, I held myself back from questioning her motivation for demanding English in the hallway. I shared how exhausting it is for me to function in my third language as a life-long English-learner myself and how refreshing it is to take a bit of a time-out from English! She nodded with understanding, so I added, just like those boys who must have needed a break from English and connect with each other in Spanish! She took a deep breath and said with compassion, "I know, I just really want them to practice English more and succeed!" I noticed the urgency with which she was ready to hurry off to where she was headed so all I had time for is to add that being bilingual is not a problem, it is such an amazing gift, it is a superpower (quoting the 12th Secretary of Education, Miguel Cordona), and invited her to join the group next time I am visiting so we could chat more about how those boys are doing!

When multilingualism is viewed a problem, we respond by naming and identifying it as such! It might begin with one conversation, with one teacher, but we must move beyond simply raising awareness and aim to eliminate harmful practices. We must *eliminate* those harmful practices and generate counter narratives that affirm and not deny multilingualism as a key dimension of one's identity. Those counter stories and counter actions are based on the two other orientations towards multilingualism, such as viewing it as a right and as an asset.

When multilingualism is viewed as a right:

- There are collaboratively developed and clearly articulated policies in place regarding multilingual rights for members of the district and school community
- All members of the local educational community have the right to use their full linguistic repertoires
- Families are fully informed in the language(s) of their choice because all essential documents are available translated to every language represented in print or digital formats
- Resources are allocated for interpreters and bilingual/multilingual family liaisons
- No one is discriminated against based on their languages or language varieties

Tapestry of Voices

Andrea Hellman, Professor of Linguistics/TESOL at Missouri State University, cautions about the difference between district- and school-level policies and emphasizes the need for school-level policy development work:

> *I have found that most schools don't have a school level service plan to serve multilingual students. They might have a district level plan, but it's not disseminated to parents, it's not disseminated to teachers, and it's not disseminated to school personnel, and all changes that happen in multilingual education is on the school level. So, we created Teams USA (Hellman, 2024) funded by a US DOE National Professional Development Grant. It is a yearlong professional development for school-based teams, focused on 10 equity principles, and we are using an equity inventory as a basis for evidence-based discussions among school teams. The school teams must have an administrator and an EL specialist and classroom teachers representing the different constituencies and the different roles in the school. And the major outcome of this PD is that schools translate their district level plan to a school level plan and actually allocate resources and train personnel to carry out the school level plan.*

When multilingualism is viewed as a resource:

- Multilingual members of the school community are valued not just for their linguistic abilities and skills but for multilingualism to be an important aspect of their heritages and identities.
- All languages and language varieties in a school community are accepted as a tool for thinking and communication.
- Multilingualism is the goal of all students and its definition might be broadened to be more inclusive.
- Multilingualism is the emerging norm in a global economy.
- See range of interpretations and contexts for multilingualism on the We Are All Multilingual website at www.wamcam.org.

Notable Research

Ester de Jong and her colleagues (2019) focus on the multilingualism-as-a-resource orientation in a study exploring its implications to dual language education, yet they suggest that the following applies to all students regardless of the program model they participate in:

> *It is neither ethical, effective, nor possible or desirable to ask students or teachers to leave their multilingual realities at the school door. In order to support multilingual students' learning and engagement in school, educators must recognize and build on what students already know and our understandings of multilingual development and learning as they develop and implement their curriculum. This premise results in an imperative to take a multilingual stance to all learning regardless of the specific program implemented for minoritized language speakers.*
>
> (de Jong et al., 2019, p. 111)

Tapestry of Voices

Jana Pridalova, EAL and English Teacher at H-Farm International School in Venice, Italy, shared her school's multifaceted view of supporting multilingual learners depicted in the diagram in Figure 3.1. She noted:

> *We view the rich linguistic backgrounds of our students as a resource—linguistically and culturally. Languages and the worlds that are created through engagement (communication, exploration of texts, cultural heritage) must be viewed as an asset and used in creative ways in classrooms to encourage students to expand on their existing knowledge.*

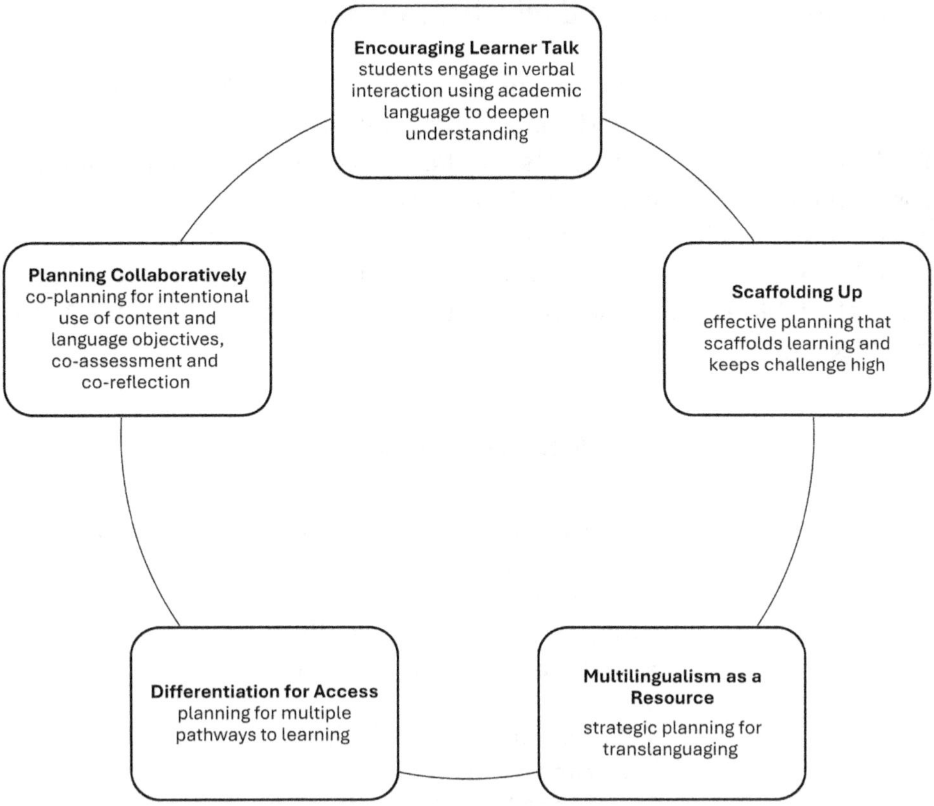

Figure 3.1 An asset-based framework for multilingualism.

Robert Sharples, Director of North Street Education and the Heddle EAL platform, also emphasizes the important role educators and especially leaders have in creating linguistically just learning environments through policies and practices:

> *In an educational context, there is much that teachers can do but the responsibility lies with leaders. We are all responsible for using our power to set expectations, create explicit policies and be accountable for multilingual justice. That persuasive and policy work is slow but essential; for me it is more important than the more visible activities that are often promoted.*

Pause for a Moment

What are your personal and professional commitments to ensure that multilingualism is not viewed as problem?

What local steps have been taken or will need to be taken to ensure it is a right and an asset?

Responding to Inequities and Injustices with Words

Whether in words or actions, "we want to reach the point where it feels more uncomfortable *not* to respond than to respond" (Gorski & Swalwell, 2023a, p. 52). Words are powerful: words are the tools educators use to plan, teach, assess, and comfort students. Words are also needed for interactions with all others—families, colleagues, supervisors, community members—in contexts ranging from participating in successful ongoing collaborations, to engaging in uncomfortable professional conversations, to taking a challenging advocacy stance.

Words Have Power

Words have power within me
Some words give me pause
Some words give me joy
Some words give me dignity
Some words take all that away

Words can show empathy
Words can reveal one's humanity
Words can take all that away

Words may carry bias, prejudice, judgment and destruction
Words may transport anger, frustration, aggression,
Words may cause and uphold oppression
Words carry power within them

Words can offer challenge or affirmation
Words can also cause disruption
Word can bring compassion, understanding, solidarity, and visibility.
Words may even show the path to dismantling injustice and inequity!

When we respond to inequities and injustices including biases and prejudices in what is being said or done in a professional setting, in the shorter term, we can choose words or actions. Let's start with words, because "staying silent in times of injustice is a privilege" (Niño & Perez-Diaz, 2021, p. 90) and in the equity work I am inviting you to join me here, silence is not an option. There is not one way or one right way to respond, so consider the following strategies as invitations. All strategies and practices could and should be adjusted to your local context and expanding to actions both in the shorter and longer terms (see more on those in Chapter 4).

Start with One Question and One Conversation

Begin small but begin somewhere! Rather than looking the other way, making assumptions, or having a ready-to-go (band-aid) solution in the form of "Yes, but …" I invite you to take a more nuanced approach to how to respond. Instead of quickly shutting down the opportunity to get to the core of the issues and working on addressing the inequities and injustices, let's start with some questions. Yet, beginning with something along the lines of "Why would you say that …?" or "How can you do that …?" will not get us too far. Feel free to generate some further questions across the various approaches I am presenting next.

The first set of questions are all yes-no questions that seem slightly more tentative and invitational, but are intended to give the original speaker an option to reflect and rephrase:

- Is it possible to view this challenge/issue differently, such as …?
- Is there another way to see that …?
- Could it be explained by …?
- Do we have enough information/evidence/data to say …?
- ______________________________
- ______________________________

The following types of questions request elaborations and more details. They are based on professional inquiry, curiosity, and a sincere desire to get to a deeper understanding of the sources of biases, inequities, or other forms of injustices that were observed or noted.

- Could you tell me more about what happened …?
- What was a specific detail that led to …?
- What are some other specific observations or concerns you have about …?
- What do others have to say about …/What have others noticed about …?
- ______________________________
- ______________________________

The next set of questions encourage perspective taking, by stepping out of your comfort zone, positioning yourself in the context of the injustice or inequity:

- If we step into the shoes of multilingual learners/families, what are their experiences with …?
- What other factors, experiences, realities are at play here that we must consider …?
- Are we creating space and opportunities to make it safe and productive to …?
- How can we build trust with others who …?
- ______________________________
- ______________________________

The final set of questions address equity issues most directly by naming what inequities or injustices were recognized:

- What are the barriers to multilingual learners …?
- How can we ensure a more equitable view of multilingual learners …?
- How can we work towards more equitable outcomes for multilingual learners when …?
- Who is or is not at the table when we discuss/make decisions about multilingual learners …?
- ______________________________
- ______________________________

Tapestry of Voices

Kathy Lobo, ESL Teacher, Brown Middle School, Newton, Massachusetts, WIDA fellow, takes a similar approach to confronting inequities:

When I see something that is inequitable or unjust, I usually pose a question to call attention to or highlight the problem or issue. For example, if a teacher complains to me that a parent of a multilingual learner has been unresponsive to emails sent by the teacher (only in English), I will ask if they have tried using the communication tools provided by the district that automatically translate messages into the home languages of our students. If a teacher needs help, I ask if I can offer some directions on how to use those tools and tips on how to communicate directly

> *and clearly with families. If my colleague does not seem to adjust their approach, I ask if they are familiar with the Title VI of the Civil Rights Act of 1964 and the Equal Education Opportunity Act of 1974, which mandate that schools communicate with parents in a language that they understand.*

Quescussions

When you looked at the heading, I bet you said something along the lines of, "Ah, a big typo! It must be Discussions, right? I reacted the same way when I first encountered this concept originally coined by Mike Johnston but introduced to me by Zoe Weil (2023), who suggests that asking the right questions and asking even more of them might just be the pathway to discovering some answers to complex interconnected issues. In a *quescussion*, a question is answered by another question, and in response, yet another question is posed, touching upon all the core interrelated concerns. Question after question, participants avoid rushing to conclusion or aiming for quick fixes. Instead, several surface and deeper level questions will emerge, including ones that begin with why and how. Multiple why's and how's are likely to get to the root of the problems or aim to uncover some hidden causes of inequities (see more on this in Chapter 4). Try this for a set length of time, such as for only about 5–8 minutes first, either in pairs or small groups, and see what emerges from this question-focused activity practiced both in sustainability education and psychology. You can treat this approach as a brief experimentation with a novel kind of discussion that is designed to break mental models, challenge preconceived notions and assumptions, and counteract cognitive biases.

Collaborative Questions and Reflections

Another way to peel back layers of understanding is to jointly reflect on and co-construct responses and next steps. Consider Table 3.2 inspired by York-Barr and colleagues' (2016) collaborative reflection framework. In this highly adapted version, we look at multilingual inequities. The four steps of the framework are designed to closely examine a particular example of inequity or injustice by (1) addressing what happened by inviting a detailed, objective description, (2) uncovering why the event took place through jointly analyzing and interpreting the details, (3) making sense of the overall meaning and impact of the event, and (4) determining implications for action.

Table 3.2 Four critical steps of collaborative reflections with guiding questions.

Steps	Key questions	Goals	Guiding questions
1	**What happened?**	Description	• What did I do? What did we do? What did others do? • What was the effect of my/our/their actions at the time? • What was the context? What was going on? Where and when did it happen? • Was there anything unusual going on at the same time?
2	**Why did it happen?**	Analysis, interpretation	• Why do I/we think the event/incident happened in this way? • How might the context have influenced the experience? • Are there other potential contributing factors? • What are my/our initial explanations about why things happened the way they did?
3	**So what?**	Overall meaning	• Why did the event/incident seem significant to reflect on? • What have I/we learned from this? • How might the event change future thinking, behaviors, or interactions? • What questions remain? What new questions emerge?
4	**Now what?**	Implications for action	• Who should be actively included in reflecting on this event? • Next time a situation like this presents itself, how do I/we want to approach it? • How can I/we set up conditions to increase the likelihood of productive interactions and learning? • What actionable next steps can be planned based on the event?

Calling In, Not Calling Out

When you hear something that bothers you, something that you know is a clear sign of prejudice, bias, or misconception and a colleague or a whole bunch of others just seem to agree, what do you do? Remaining silent is not an option, but confronting colleagues head on could be just as counterproductive by shutting critical conversations down before they even began. I first heard an interview with Loretta Ross in late 2021 on an NPR talk show, and I was immediately taken by what she referred to as using "radical empathy" to engage in difficult conversations with others, rather than react and publicly humiliate them. To counteract "cancel culture" or "call-out culture," she defines "calling in is really a call-out done with love. So, it's the same thing, but instead of using anger, blaming and shaming as your method of achieving accountability, you use love, grace and respect" (TED Radio Hour, 2021). I applied Loretta Ross's (2025) five-step approach (p. 157) to *calling in* when responding to inequities in multilingual contexts in the moment through words:

1 ***Start with the self.*** Show your vulnerability and share one of your own experiences with a similar challenge you are responding to; express a feeling that you used to harbor, offer a quick personal anecdote related to the situation, make it personally relevant and relatable.
2 ***Calibrate the conflict.*** Remind yourself that most issues will not be resolved in a single conversation so pace yourself at the unset of the conversation and quietly reflect on what might be some achievable goals for the current conversation. As Glenn Singleton (2021) also suggests, we must accept non-closure when we participate in courageous conversations, while also advancing the equity work, we are committed to.
3 ***Approach with love.*** As you engage in the conversation, check yourself for any signs of frustration and keep your goal in mind: it is all about the students and the care and love multilingual learners deserve.
4 ***Accept the reaction.*** You do not have to agree with what you hear but show your appreciation for the vulnerability that was shared and honesty that was demonstrated without a personal attack.
5 ***Reach a resolution.*** Discuss ideas and actions, not individuals. Propose actionable next steps.

Pause for a Moment

As you reviewed the five steps, have you visualized yourself in an equity situation where you wanted to call someone out but now you would rather try calling them in?
Consider Loretta Ross's guidance (Ross, 2025, p. 79). How do you seek "power with" instead of "power over" others?

Establishing and Following Collaboration Norms

Developing collaborative practices in support of understanding and responding to the complex needs of culturally and linguistically diverse student body remains urgent. What Andy Hargreaves concluded after reviewing 30 years of research on collaboration continues to hold true.

> *We are in a period of educational change when collaboration seems to have become the answer to almost everything. If collaborative efforts prove insufficient for or ineffective in the face of the complex challenges we now face of deeper learning and greater wellbeing, then teachers will retreat back to their own classrooms, and policy makers will return to top-down solutions. It is important now, therefore, not just that teachers collaborate, but that they collaborate well, and that school and system leaders enable and empower them to do that.*
>
> (Hargreaves, 2019, p. 618)

Uncovering and responding to inequities and injustices impacting multilingual learners cannot be assigned or taken up by any one person. It needs to be a collaborative effort that requires many stake holders to work together and the complex relationships and interactions among them to be productive. I adapted the seven norms of collaboration originally established by Robert J. Garmston and Bruce M. Wellman (2016).

1. ***Pausing.*** When pausing before responding to a challenge or situation, or before asking a question, you prevent a knee-jerk reaction or rush, impulsive rejoinder. You give yourself some wait time, it may just ensure a moment of thoughtful reflection, which in turn will adjust the pace for the discussion.
2. ***Paraphrasing.*** When you restate in your own words what was just spoken, you stay focused on what was just shared rather than switching to some new ideas abruptly. Paraphrasing that begins with "I think I heard you say …" or "Let me see if I understood it correctly …" or "Could we confirm that we are all on the same page when it comes to …" not only gives opportunities for clarifications, but also ensures shared meaning-making among all members of the group. Paraphrasing lends new voices and words to the first speaker's ideas, thus enhancing transparency and consistency in the conversation.
3. ***Posing questions.*** As discussed before, posing questions is a critical part of developing deeper understanding and making responses more insightful. Asking questions further adjusts the dynamic between

speakers and listeners, since there is dedicated time for further exploring assumptions, reducing ambiguity, and seeking clarity.

4. ***Putting ideas on the table ideas.*** Presenting additional ideas and inviting divergent perspectives contribute to meaningful discussions that recognize the complexity of injustices and inequities. Sharing new ideas works best when all participants understand that these collaborative conversations must take place without fear of embarrassment or retribution.
5. ***Providing data.*** Offering data or evidence of the inequities and injustices enhances the overall collaborative process. Both qualitative and quantitative data should be welcome for the group to explore. Through careful collaborative analysis and interpretation, critical, well-informed next steps can be determined.
6. ***Paying attention to self and others.*** Throughout the entire collaborative process, members of the group remain attentive to their own and others' participation, which includes not just what is being said but how it is being shared. Verbal and nonverbal communication moves, body language, gestures, tone of voice (and much more) all contribute to developing awareness of how the conversation is going.
7. ***Presuming positive intentions.*** Even during the most challenging professional conversations or interactions, our assumptions that everyone's intentions are positive and professional will keep the dialogue on track. In a healthy work environment, disagreements are considered a natural part of the collaborative process with participating educators focusing on productive problem solving and collective efficacy.

Tapestry of Voices

Ruslana Westerlund, educational consultant and researcher, shared her approach to responding to multilingual inequities, reiterating the importance of several aspect of these noms of collaboration:

Have the courage to interrupt and the inquiry to come from the place of curiosity and not judgment. Ask clarifying questions. Name the impact, not the intent. Therefore, the group agreement "Presume positive intent" should be followed with "but own your impact." It is not only the intent that matters but if the impact of our words or actions causes harm, we must own it.

Pause for a Moment

What do you do when words cannot take you far enough in your equity work?

How do you handle frustrating conversations or avoidance behavior?

Responding with Immediate or Short-Term Actions

Just as responses in words, responses as actions will also vary based on the context, the situation that was observed and noted, the injustice and inequity that was uncovered, and many other variables. As noted in Chapter 2, shadowing protocols, equity audits and other equity-oriented activities and practices will help recognize what individual cases or persistent patterns of inequities are present. Raising awareness is critical but will not suffice. Immediate and short-term responses in action may be directly connected to two key equity principles: prioritization and just access. More specially, when responding to inequities through immediate actions, we commit to (a) prioritizing the needs of multilingual learners and (b) ensuring that all students including multilingual learners have access to both tangible and intangible resources (Gorski & Swalwell, 2023a).

Show Sincere Concern and Extend Care

When multilingual learners and their families experience bias, prejudice, discrimination, or any other form of inequity or injustice, they might or might not always be fully aware of what has happened or what is happening. After recognizing multilingual inequities and injustices, as equity literate educators, we might take note of the instance, the persons involved, the intent and the impact of the communication. So, let's show our care and concern to the students and their families by addressing the inequities in meetings, in written communications, in action plans across all aspects of students' education, including inequities in curriculum, instruction and assessment (see Chapter 4 for more on those three aspects of multilingual learners' educational experiences).

Be the Learner

Education matters! As educators, form professional learning groups (study groups, inquiry groups) that commit to learning more about languages, bilingualism, multilingualism and multilingual learners' academic, linguistic, and social emotional needs. There are many choices to explore ranging from reading, studying, and applying the lessons from a single, carefully selected, professional journal magazine article (see for example, *English Teaching Professional*, *Language Magazine*, *TESOL Journal*, special topic issues of *Educational Leadership* to name a few) to engaging in year-long equity journeys and everything in between.

Notable Research

Christy Wessel-Powell, Alexandra Panos and Regina Weir (2021) documented a long term-effort to ensure equity is a shared purpose. Their Year of Equity (YoE) was designed as a community-led school equity literacy campaign with the goals of establishing critical literacy practice and advocacy:

> *The YoE offers lessons for critical equity literacy in communities contending with the confluence of affluence, Whiteness and inequity in public schools. [The study focused on] democratically designed public events held over 1 year (e.g. book clubs, public forums and action committee meetings) as iterative critical literacy invitations and actions to engage community members in problem-solving the issue of school inequity.*
>
> (Wessel-Powell et al., 2021, p. 62)

During the COVID-19 pandemic, I often found myself on Zoom or Google Meet. One of the silver-linings of the lockdown was to witness and support how educators created their own professional support systems and PLNs (Personal Learning Networks). Digital platforms, social media tools, blogs, YouTube channels, all helped educators connect locally, regionally, and even globally. I was invited numerous times to help launch book studies based on some of my publications or appear for Q&As at the end of these online discussions. While the COVID crisis ended a few years ago, grassroots efforts to get together on Zoom or Google to discuss professional challenges ebbed, the interest in continued shared learning has remained. Locally facilitated book clubs or educator-initiated book studies have been recognized by school and district leaders across the country as valuable, meaningful professional learning opportunities that may build deeper understanding of multilingualism while also enhancing teacher agency and ownership of their own learning. Book studies may last for several weeks or months and can be connected to shared explorations of multilingual practices that live not just on the pages of the books but in the classrooms, too. See the textbox on page 70 for a short list of recommended books for shared exploration of multilingualism and policies and practices that support multilingual learners.

Recommended Book List for Shared Professional Learning

Auslander, L., & Yip, J. (2022). *School-wide systems for multilingual learner success: A roadmap for leaders*. Routledge.

Dove, M. G., Honigsfeld, A., & McDermott Goldman, C. (2025). *Nine dimensions of scaffolding for multilingual learners*. Corwin.

Ernst-Slavit, G., & Gottlieb, M. (2026). *Academic languaging: Engaging multilingual students in content area learning*. Corwin.

García, O., Kleifgen, J. A., & Cervantes-Soon, C. (2025). *Educating emergent bilinguals: Policies, programs, and practices for multilingual learners* (3rd edition). Teachers College Press.

Gottlieb, M. (2024). *Assessing multilingual learners: Bridges to empowerment* (3rd edition). Corwin.

Honigsfeld, A. (2019). *Growing academic language and literacy: Strategies for English learners* (Grades K-8). Heinemann.

Honigsfeld, A. (2024). *Growing language and literacy* (Grades 6–12). Heinemann.

Singer, T. W. (2025). *Accelerating language and literacy: The flip-to guide to multilingual learner excellence in the core* (2nd edition). Corwin.

Walqui, A., Bunch, G. C., & Mueller, P. (Eds.). *Amplifying the curriculum: Designing quality learning opportunities for multilingual learners* (2nd edition). Teachers College Press.

Zwiers, J. (2024). *Overhauling learning for multilingual students: An approach for achieving pedagogical justice*. Corwin.

Let Multilingual Learners Be the Teachers

I often challenge educators to learn at least 20 sentences in every language spoken in their classrooms. Start simple, with *Hello*'s and *How are you*'s and move to more complex sentences and sentiments such as *I am happy to see you in class today*! With the rapid advancement of AI in recent years, having accurate reliable translations are getting easier and more convenient by the day. Yet, the best teachers of these powerful statements will be your students themselves. When the power dynamic changes and students become the experts and the knowers, their status and the importance of their languages are elevated. Suddenly, it is going to the teachers who struggle with pronunciation, who keep forgetting phrases in an unfamiliar language, who mix up word order, and so on. The goal is not for the teachers to develop advanced communicative competence in a range of languages, yet the message is clear! Students' languages matter! Their multilingualism matters and as a result, the students matter!

Publicly Validate Multilingualism and Multilingual Learners

Even though there are a number of designated opportunities to celebrate Hispanic Heritage Month (September 15–October 15) or Asian American Pacific Islander Heritage Month (May), or to acknowledge International Mother Language Day (February 21) in many places expanded as the Mother Language Week or recognize the importance of National Bilingual/Multilingual Learner Advocacy Month (April), these days, weeks, or even entire months rarely move beyond raising awareness. A heroes and holidays approach (Banks, 2019) will not offer equity-focused responses to the core challenges multilingual families and students face. Instead, we need to move multilingualism and multilingual students, and all those associated with them from the margins to the center and tell their stories. Collecting, sharing, and retelling stories of survival and resilience, stories of being culture and language brokers; stories of developing literacy in multiple places and multiple languages; stories of students we know and care about may change hearts and minds, and may even impact policies and practices.

Many educators I have worked with and whose dedication to multilingualism and multilingual learners also create locally published collections of stories. Susan Rosato, secondary ELD teacher at Colchester High School, Vermont, WIDA fellow, compiles her students' essays into annual digital publications that are shared with faculty. The stories are also published in hardcover books that students get to keep and share with their families. Susan's students also collaborate with a sixth-grade general education class, where the students lead group discussions and share their stories with an authentic audience. See an excerpt below from one of her students' stories written when he was in 9th grade, titled "Not Always Sunshine and Rainbows." The segment shared here focuses on his language-related experiences.

Not Always Sunshine and Rainbows

When I first arrived in the United States, my mind was altered with foolish and unrealistic thoughts. I thought life in the USA was the best life you could possibly have; I thought that you didn't have to strive to be great in the Land of Patriotism. I thought everything would be handed to me if I just said so; I thought I finally made it.

The first couple of days were sweet and easy. As a little black African kid, my eyes widened at the fact that schools here are way different than in my home country, Burkina Faso. Kids would misbehave, be loud, and talk back to teachers, and there would be no repercussions. Instead, the teacher would say to go to the corner of the room and stare at a blank wall until you're ready to calm down. The discipline applied in my country compared to the USA would be a swift and humiliating pain on your buttocks. The language barrier between me and my peers blocked my path from feeling a part of the new community. I wanted to speak, but my tongue was caught in a knot. I wanted to express my feelings, but my feelings could not be transmitted out of me, so instead, I ended up alone and wondering if I would ever be able to communicate in English.

Another challenge I faced was seeing how cold people really are. For example, someone would seem so kind, but later, you discover they are two-faced. Burkina Faso means land of the honest and land of integrity and I carried that with me because I found it to be beautiful. Seeing people act in negative ways influenced and affected my thinking and gave me a nasty stereotype. At first, I had the idea that Americans were idols, essentially icons, but that changed when I was introduced to racism. The reason why I say this is because when I was younger, a peer told me to say a racist slur and said it was a good thing. As a young kid then, I didn't know what it meant, and I wanted to fit in, so I said it to a teacher, and she gasped surprisingly and told me to leave the classroom. I was puzzled, confused, embarrassed, and I was ashamed. I later found out that it was a bitter racist slur and should never be used.

I realized America wasn't really all sunshine and rainbows. At the young age of 9, I learned that things would not be handed down to me if I said so. I knew I had to work at least twice as hard as other students around me to be at their level or better. I was comparing myself to my peers, and I was behind. I told myself that I would never be behind again, and I bested some of the students in the class and kept working, upholding myself to a higher standard.

I know more challenges will come, and I'm fine with that because it will make me stronger and build my character.

The power of storytelling is at the core of a few of the exceptional examples I have come across over the years, as listed below.

- **Published resources:**
  - Emily Francis's memoir told as letters to her students in *If Only You Knew* (2022)
  - Emily Francis's *Millie's Journey* Series (2025)
  - Andrea Bitner's students' inspiring true stories in *Take Me Home* (2025) and *When Niagara Falls* (2025)

- Helen Thorpe's account of 22 teenagers throughout an academic year in Denver Public Schools: *The Newcomers: Finding Refuge, Friendship, and Hope in America* (2018)
- Ali Abu Zeid's memoir where voice is a metaphor for all his struggles in *The Weight of My Voice: A Refugee's Journey Through Silence, Struggle, and Strength* (2025)

◆ **Digital resources:**
- I Learn America—https://ilearnamerica.com
- Immigrant Stories—www.immigrantdefenseproject.org/immigrant-stories
- The Immigrant Story—https://theimmigrantstory.org
- We Are America Project—www.weareamericaproject.com

◆ **TED Talks** offered by bilingual and multilingual youths ranging from 3rd grade to high school on the benefits, challenges and unique context of their multilingualism:
- *How Multilingualism Helps Me Navigate the World* by Soundarya Lahari Keesara (TEDxHaarlem Youth)—www.youtube.com/watch?v=4uKMAyz4MIM
- *The Benefits of Being Bilingual* by Bella Lawson & Jose Sabedra (TEDxKids@ElCajon)—www.youtube.com/watch?v=eAqVR4JQITc
- *The Story Behind a Multilingual Brain* by Hannah Jung (TEDxYantai Huasheng International School)—www.youtube.com/watch?v=y84KxzA5xrI
- *Multilingualism and Its Impact* by Srishti Gotam (TEDxYouth@Evans)—www.youtube.com/watch?v=bxpnruRkADE

Notable Research

Jennifer Burton explored Critical Multilingual Language Awareness (CMLA) through spoken word poetry with learners from refugee backgrounds. She positioned students' lives and languages at the center of critical language learning and found that her study participants "disrupted deficit narratives of refugees as illegitimate and reclaimed their right to be heard, seen and felt, first and foremost, as humans" (Burton, 2025, p. 2179). The study also concluded that "bearing witness to students' memories and stories facilitates a process of cocreation of new memories and experiences with transformative potential, which become realized in between the self and others" (p. 2191). The powerful practical implications remind us to invite language learning opportunities that connect emotions and student identities into our classrooms.

Spotlight on Multilingual Justice

Let's hear from Sarah Whitfield, District ML Instructional Specialist & Summer Newcomer Academy Director, in Cabarrus County Schools, North Carolina, about how the theme of "Our Stories Belong Here" became central to the entire program:

> We were finishing up the first week of the Summer Newcomer Academy. This first week was intentionally designed to weave our theme, "Our Stories Belong Here" into every part of our program–caregiver collaboration, team-building activities, guest speakers and instruction. We wanted students to understand the purpose of our program. But more importantly, we wanted them to experience a true sense of belonging in their schools and new community going into a new school year.
>
> On the first day, I told students "You belong here. Your journey matters. Cabarrus County Schools are better because YOU are in it." I wanted these words to be more than a welcome message; I wanted students to internalize them. Throughout the week I looked for evidence that the message and my team's meticulous planning was taking root. Were students smiling, laughing, connecting with each other, or their teachers? Most students were initially reluctant at first, but day by day I could see how we were slowly creating a small community. Each day I heard more multilingual chatter, laughter and saw smiles. I could sense their confidence growing. They were slowly warming up to each other and us.
>
> One student in particular, Luis, was especially quiet and hesitant to share and engage during our morning team building activities, lunch, and during most instruction. He arrived in the United States from El Salvador the previous August. He was at the "entering" level of English language proficiency across all domains. However, speaking and writing domains were particularly challenging for him. It was clear to me that he needed structured language support and a safe invitation for him to share about himself and his experiences.
>
> Luis was in one of the classrooms that I stepped into for a quick check-in. As I observed the lesson, I noticed a quiet, but powerful moment unfolding. The previous day, the teacher read aloud "Same, Same But Different" by Jenny Sue Kostecki-Shaw. Students were completing an "Identity Wheel" for themselves after the teacher had modeled her own. Their assignment was to complete

their own identity wheel listing the most important aspects of their identity. This "wheel" would then be used as an anchor for a paragraph explaining how their values and beliefs contribute to their identity.

On the walls, I saw chart paper with a word bank, a completed identity wheel, a paragraph frame, and the mentor text displayed. (ML teachers are the only people I know that can take an empty, bare classroom and make the walls ooze language. It's their superpower!) The teacher was modeling how to complete the diagram with the students. She clarified some words and concepts in their first language.

I walked towards Luis's desk. He was quietly writing as he looked at the teacher's example, so he could carefully craft his own. He thoughtfully sketched the icons for family, education, language and hobbies. At the top of the page he wrote "One important part of my identity is my family because I love them so much." He wrote this using the sentence frame provided by the teacher. Students were then asked to talk with a partner about how their values were similar and different to each other. He spoke freely, referring to the sentence frame, expressing that he and another classmate both shared the same emphasis and value for education. Through his writing I was able to learn that he has a deep love and respect for his family, and values honesty in himself and others. He has an adventurous spirit, and believes in his own power. Over the course of the program, he grew in confidence, comfortability and a sense of belonging began to emerge. He even opened up and shared that he wants to work in the hospitality industry as a future career.

I left the room with a deeper understanding of why identity work and storytelling matters with multilingual learners. When students are given safe spaces to share their stories, with structure and support, they can freely share what they may be holding inside. For me, this is when our theme of "Our Stories Belong Here" and my welcome message of "You belong here. Your journey matters. Cabarrus County Schools are better because YOU are in it" went from simple words to a powerful instructional practice. The theme of our first week took root with this writing activity. When students feel seen and valued for who they are, a true sense of belonging begins to grow.

Pause for a Moment

How did the summer program change the narrative about multilingual learners, in this case, about newcomers?

What similar initiatives are you familiar with or would you like to plan and implement?

Legitimize Multilingualism in All Learning Spaces and Learning Opportunities

My call to action is to transform the learning environment (the various physical locations in the school) and all educational opportunities students engage in to invite, fully accept and affirm multilingualism. "Rather than framing students' uses of [their home languages] as markers of deficiency, teachers can recognize, praise, and investigate student language use to inform classroom meaning-making" (Pacheco et al., 2019, p. 77). When multilingual participation in learning is not viewed as an oddity, something to frown upon and correct, it begins to occupy a legitimate place in classrooms, in curricula, in learning activities, in assessment practices.

The shorter-term responses usually rest on the shoulders of equity-oriented, advocacy-minded teachers or leaders who introduce linguistically responsive and sustaining pedagogy into their daily routines. More longer-term approaches will be discussed in subsequent chapters.

Tapestry of Voices

Aradhana Mudambi, founder of Language & Equity, offers her insights into why responding to inequities is challenging and what we can do about it. It is most fitting to end this chapter and bridge into the next one with her words. Unity and leadership are critical elements of not only promptly and effectively responding to inequities but to addressing them in the longer term as well:

> *We live in a society where people are scared to respond to biases. Educators need the professional development to be able to respond. We need to build unity across educational institutions to be able to push back against current inequities. And we need to have a group planning responses and serving as a leader in this work.*

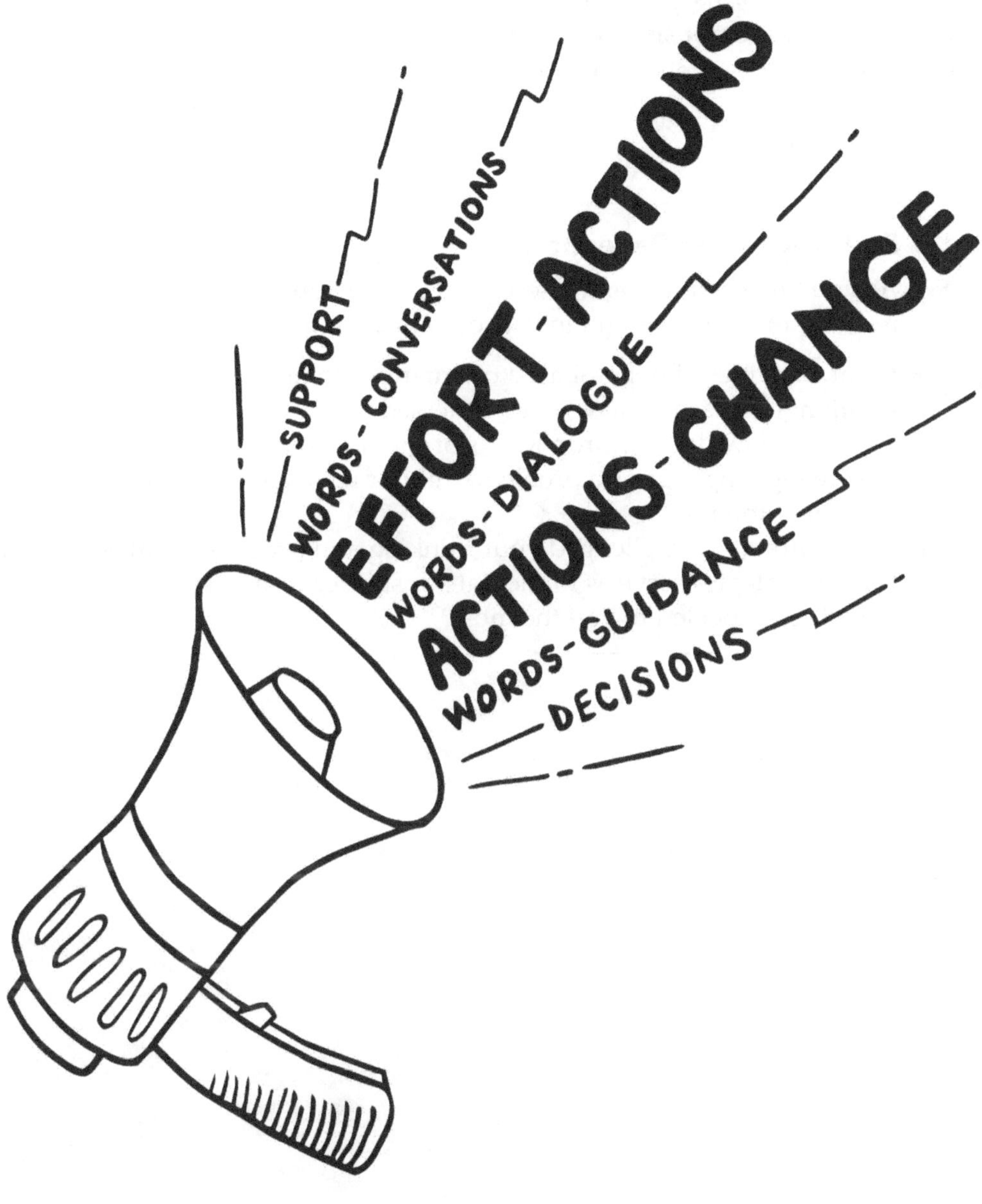
SUPPORT
WORDS - CONVERSATIONS
EFFORT - ACTIONS
WORDS - DIALOGUE
ACTIONS - CHANGE
WORDS - GUIDANCE
DECISIONS

Moving Beyond Responding to Multilingual Inequities

Responding to multilingual inequities and injustices in words and implementing immediate, short-term actions are more than temporary fixes, or quick interventions; as presented in this chapter, they require skills and practice. Yet they are not sufficient to ensure lasting impact. The next chapter continues in the same vein of addressing multilingual injustices but focuses on long-term next steps to be able to get to the root causes of the inequities and redress them.

End-of-Chapter Reflections

As you finish exploring the second ability of equity literacy, to respond to inequities and injustices, reflect on the following:

- What examples of deficit-based orientations to multilingualism and multilingual learners have you witnessed?
- Why and how does Ricardo Ruíz's original tri-part policy framework of viewing language as a problem, right or resource continue to be important today?
- Which strategies challenged your thinking and practice the most?
- Which strategies serve as immediate or shorter-term responses to inequities appealed to you the most?

4

How to Redress Multilingual Inequities and Injustices

So Much More

When we become aware of and recognize inequities and injustices
connected to multilingualism, we notice them, name them,
identify them, describe them, deeply reflect on them, yet we can
do so much more!

When we respond to inequities and injustices by speaking up,
we give words to our observations and concerns, we verbally note
our discomfort, we challenge discriminatory language or behavior in
ourselves and others, we engage in empowering conversations, yet we
can do so much more!

When we respond to inequities with immediate actions, we offer
support to those who were wronged and suffered prejudice
or discrimination, we seek out and begin to use resources
that provide access to multilingual learners, we educate
ourselves and keep learning about multilingualism, yet we can
do so much more!

We can do so much more!
Do so much more!
Much more!

DOI: 10.4324/9781003644071-4

In the previous chapters, we established some emerging, yet critical early practices to bring about multilingual justice in the educational context through recognizing and responding to inequities. Doing so in the moment or the short term will likely contribute to raising awareness, initiating conversations that have not happened before, beginning to change minds and hearts and shifting the climate of a classroom, a grade level, a school or a district. Changing the culture, the way we do things in this school, district or community, is another matter! Just to clarify how I use some terms here:

- **Culture** is defined by the values and beliefs that determine the overall identity of an educational place. It is the fabric of an institution that implicitly tells its members how to behave and what to do in certain situations, what the norms and expectations are.
- **Climate**, on the other hand, refers to how members of that same community feel or are made to feel, what the overarching mood or atmosphere is in that place. The climate seems to be more malleable and easier to change especially with new leadership, some important events that take place, or when new policies are introduced and observed.

Changing the underlying culture of a place will require more consistent and persistent effort, and likely more time. Steve Gruenert and Todd Whitaker (2024) liken a change in culture to a slow revolution, whereas a change in climate may happen instantly. They also remind us that "if culture is a school's personality, climate is its attitude. The biggest difference between the two is that an attitude is far easier to change than a personality" (p. 11), yet the climate may also be perceived as the reflection of the underlying culture.

What is necessary and urgent is to get to the core of the matter. Why are we doing what we are doing? What in the past got us here? What is our most accurate status? Where do we want to go in the future?

We need a deeper understanding of the causes of the inequities and injustices so they could be eradicated as well as identifying, designing, and committing to long-term, pervasive changes to policies and practices. In the first half of this chapter, I invite you to investigate the root causes of multilingual inequities with me, whereas the latter half of the chapter presents actionable next steps to redress inequities.

PROFESSIONAL LEARNING
INSTRUCTION
CURRICULUM
ASSESSMENT
MULTI-LINGUAL EQUITY AUDIT
STUDENT SEGREGATION
MONOLINGUAL BIAS
DISCRIMINATORY ASSESSMENTS
PEDAGOGICAL INJUSTICE
ENGLISH-ONLY POLICIES

Investigating the Root Causes of Multilingual Inequities

Have you tried some practices suggested in Chapters 2 and 3 (be it reflections, shadowing protocols, or multilingual equity walks)? If not yet, I urge you not to miss out by skipping over these earlier equity abilities discussed in Chapters 2 and 3. If you have tried some, you might have taken copious notes, gathered some illuminating observation data, and gained ample experience addressing inequities in the immediate term. To further investigate and determine what underlying factors lead to inequities, however, a more thorough analysis is required. Let's explore some options and the anticipated outcomes of these essential equity practices.

Equity Audit

Equity audits typically focus on policies, programs, or instructional and assessment practices that disproportionately impact specific subgroups of students, such as a multilingual learners. Audits may also uncover the discriminatory effects on students' families and other school community members related to dimensions of diversity such as race, ethnicity, gender or gender identity, sexual orientation, dis/ability, age, religion, socio-economic status, or other factors. Equity audits peel back layers of evidence that emerge from multiple sources of data. The overarching purpose is not just to identify disparities, inequities, and inconsistencies that might not have been noticeable without collecting a wide range of data and systematically analyzing them but to address them with principled long-term actions.

There are a variety of data collection or analysis methods, protocols, or sets of questions or data sources to conduct an equity audit (see for example, Green, 2017; Palmer et al., 2019a; Staehr-Fenner, n.d.). There is not one standard template or a single formula to uncover all the challenges and inequities that any groups of students might experience so no such tool exists for multilingual learners. Inspired by the core phases Colleen Capper and colleagues (2020) outlined, I further adapted a protocol I previously created with Audrey Cohan (Honigsfeld & Cohan, 2024) and added some specific recommendations as tips to keep in mind. As with all other tools and protocols in this book, I encourage you to use this protocol as a possibility or a springboard and expand or reduce steps or add or omit elements of it to be more feasible in your own context.

Multilingual Equity Audit

Step 1: Establish a task force or collaborative team that will design, conduct the multilingual equity audit, and analyze the findings.

Tips: Make sure a range of expertise and experiences are represented on the team. If the team needs external expertise, include a consultant as a team member.

Step 2: Identify the 6 Ps of the Multilingual Equity Audit, most or all of which are frequently included in equity audits.

Tips: The 6 Ps will help anchor the audit and provide clarity of the process, but feel free to make adjustments if needed:

- ★ *Purpose:* What is the overarching purpose and what are the specific objectives with this audit?
- ★ *Programs:* Which program or programs serving multilingual learners will the team focus on?
- ★ *People:* Who will be interviewed or otherwise approached to provide data? Whose experiences are focused upon through the audit?
- ★ *Places:* What locations (schools, classrooms, etc.) will be visited, if any?
- ★ *Policies:* What type of policies (such as federal, state, district, school, and their implementation) will be examined?
- ★ *Practices:* What program specific curricular, instructional, assessment, and other practices are going to be examined?

Step 3: Design the protocol for the audit: identify data sources and data collection methods.

Tips: While the team might be interested in using a wide range of data sources, it is important to make sure the audit is doable within a reasonable timeframe and actionable decisions can be made once the findings are available. A successful audit allows teachers to highlight areas of change that directly impact their students, especially multilingual learners (see Table 4.1).

Step 4: Collect the data.

Tips: Qualitative data collection such as interviews and focus groups will take a significantly longer time than quantitative data collection that includes demographic and assessment data and could be augmented with surveys with rating scales.

Step 5: Analyze the data by identifying trends and patterns both in qualitative and quantitative findings and interpret the findings by including school members beyond the task force.

Tips: Make sure the analysis reports on all the areas of strengths and not just gaps, shortcomings, inequities, or needs. Examine aggregated and disaggregated data for more nuanced interpretations. Look out for possible unanticipated findings, too. This is an opportunity to examine issues of disproportionality (e.g., under-, over-, and mis-representation of multilingual learners in certain programs).

Step 6: Investigate the underlying causes of the patterns and systematic trends you uncovered.

Tips: Pay close attention to disparities among groups and include multiple stakeholders to offer their perspectives.

Step 7: Identify a comprehensive set of goals based on the findings.

Tips: Consider short-term and long-term goals that are actionable, measurable, and are closely aligned with the original purpose of the equity audit. Continue to take an asset-based approach and identify opportunities for growth and change based on the results. Use these goals to help educators understand how and when they contribute to disparities faced by multilingual learners.

Step 8: Develop an action plan based on your priorities.

Tips: Challenge assumptions for preconceived notions; instead, have evidence-based conversations. Reach beyond the equity audit team members or the task force as you develop your plan to respond to the findings of the equity audit. Include a timeline for periodically revisiting the priorities and evaluating the outcomes of the changes. This is also an opportunity to highlight needs of teachers in terms of professional development. Make sure there is a feedback loop, so teachers of multilingual learners find out about accomplishments and successes made over time on behalf of their students.

Source: adapted from Honigsfeld & Cohan (2024)

The core premise of an equity audit, such as this one is to initiate and engage in it with genuine intent to uncover deep-rooted inequities and their underlying causes while remaining objective and withholding judgment. The entire process is ***built on trust*** that is already established in an educational context and is intended ***to build trust*** further. Rather than merely looking for what is wrong and finding fault or pointing fingers, the audit is meant to lead to more clearly seeing systemic barriers to multilingual learners' language, literacy and academic growth and to commit to removing them.

What Multilingual Equity Audits Might Reveal

The equity audit is likely to uncover complex results that are unique to your own context. Based on my field experience as well as the outcomes of the Delphi Panel's surveys, focus group discussions, and interviews, your findings might fit into one or more of the specific areas suggested in Table 4.1. There are some rows in each area of concern intentionally left blank so you can add your own specific findings that require further attention. Your summary

Table 4.1 Areas of concern potentially revealed by multilingual equity audits.

Major areas of concern	Specific issues requiring attention
Policies	English-only policies; separation of languages; translanguaging, grading
	Designated schools to house multilingual learners, forced removal of students from neighborhood schools
Programs	English Language Development programs that segregate students
	Academic tracking that places students in lower-level or remedial courses
	Lack of appropriate Dual Language Bilingual Education programs, or lack of access to existing ones
	Overrepresentation of multilingual learners in special education programs
	Limited access to extracurricular or enrichment programs for multilingual learners
	Limited access of multilingual learners to gifted and talented classes
Pedagogy	Lower expectations, simplifying materials and tasks, reducing rigor; no opportunities for student interaction
	Lack of culturally and linguistically responsive and sustaining curricula
	High Quality Instructional Materials only available in English
	Limited attention to oracy development and student-student interaction

(Continued)

Table 4.1 Areas of concern potentially revealed by multilingual equity audits. (Continued)

Major areas of concern	Specific issues requiring attention
Multilingual learner experiences	Attendance patterns (absenteeism)
	Disciplinary actions and suspensions
	Dropout rates
	Mobility
Assessment	Monolingual high-stakes assessments
	Over-, under-, or misidentification of multilingual learners for special education services
	Dismal graduation rates (aging out of high school without having enough credits)
	Absence of a balanced assessment system
Professional learning	Bias in hiring practices (lack of bilingual faculty and staff) and inadequate new teacher induction
	Inadequate initial teacher preparation
	Inequities in literacy-focused professional learning
	Absence of on-going professional development about multilingualism, language and literacy development
	Lack of teacher collaboration
	Lack of or limited leadership preparation for multilingual justice

(Continued)

Table 4.1 Areas of concern potentially revealed by multilingual equity audits. (Continued)

Major areas of concern	Specific issues requiring attention
Family engagement	Culturally biased and linguistically exclusive family events
	Lack of translations or interpreters
	Lack of adequate communication with families
	Lack of bilingual family liaisons as cultural brokers
	Lack of attention to families' funds of knowledge
Add on your own	

table may contain fewer items, or it may be further expanded as suggested by the outcomes of the audit conducted in your context.

The goal is not only to get a comprehensive picture about the inequities and injustices multilingual learners might have encountered, but also to gain clarity about the most pressing issues and to get the roots of what had been overlooked in the past. A closer examination of the root causes of language-based biases, discrimination, injustice, silencing of multilingual learners will be critical to grow as equity literate educators.

Pause for a Moment

Reviewing Table 4.1 alone might be overwhelming. Take it in strides but persevere! Share the task with colleagues. Once you have your areas of concern not only identified but connected to real-life data, the conversation is likely to tackle the following questions and many more.
What are the most prevalent patterns that emerged?
What plausible explanations may be provided for the data trends?
How are you and your team members planning to address them?
How might you reverse the pattern so that it becomes assets-based?

Tapestry of Voices

Ayanna Cooper, a consultant and author, cautions about taking a nuanced, justice-oriented approach to equity audits and to act on the results with accountability:

The redress is very important because it comes from a place of taking responsibility. Some key questions to consider are: (1) How are learning communities using equity audits to not only be compliant but to recreate learning communities for all learners? (2) Who is at the table? Who owns the table? Why are those impacted most not decision makers? (3) Does everyone know and accept that anti-blackness is part of linguistic justice? To say that it is not, that race is separate from linguistic justice efforts, is evidence that the field has missed the point entirely.

Ready

Eyes are open to see
Ears are open to hear
Hearts are open to care
Minds are open to understand
Hands are ready to act
Feet are ready to take the next step

Root Causes

Each school district and even each school within a district operates as a unique microcosm or ecosystem with variables ranging from size to demographics, from program models to funding sources, and from geographic location to core philosophy. There are no two identical contexts and there are no uniform solutions to fighting multilingual inequities and injustices. So, my goal is not to dispense prepackaged analyses of what any multilingual equity audit might reveal; instead, my intent is to highlight possible directions your analysis might take you and your team to reach a deeper understanding of what is happening in your local context and why inequities and injustices may persist.

Monolingual Bias and English-Only (Written, Spoken, and Unspoken) Policies

In educational settings, the monolingual mindset prioritizes English language development and mastery of what is often referred to as academic English.

This deficit-oriented view defines success predominantly, or in some cases exclusively, in terms of what is demonstrated in English. It values the progress speakers of all other languages demonstrate in not just acquiring English but in assimilating into the English-speaking academic and societal culture. At the same time, monolingual bias limits the opportunities multilingual learners have to fully develop their language and literacy skills in their home languages or to demonstrate their understanding and expertise when their full linguistic repertoires and multilingual skills and competencies are not honored. It may also prevent students from remaining connected to their heritage languages and cultures and prevent families from connecting with the schools. It may result in erasure of students' and their families' linguistic identities and lead to language-based insecurities. Within this context, "native speakerism" (which means a native speaker is perceived to be the idealized person, educator, user of a particular language) is one additional equity trap, which discriminates against those for whom English is a second or additional language.

Tapestry of Voices

Laura Ascenzi-Moreno, Professor of Bilingual Education & Bilingual Program Coordinator, Brooklyn College, cautions about the dangers of favoring monolingualism and how it contributes to multilingual injustice.

> *Multilingual injustice is when monolingual practices suppress multilingual students' language practices or students' meaning-making because students' language resources are not accepted within a school setting.*

Joan Lachance, Associate Professor of Education and Program Director of the undergraduate and graduate Teaching English as a Second Language (TESL) programs at UNC Charlotte, describes several ways monolingual bias continues to be enacted in schools:

> *When English-only environments imply intelligence only when "enough English" is demonstrated; when communities are asked to erase their multilingualism and replace their identities with English as the only language that matters; when students are denied opportunities to utilize their full linguistic repertoires during each learning experience; when students [people] are shamed for not knowing English; and, finally, when educators who are obliged to know what's beneficial for students operate from misguided positions to push for English-only agendas.*

Notable Research

Based on her extensive ethnographic fieldwork and autobiographical explorations, Lillian Ardell (2025) documents why and how monolingual bias can be disrupted. In her framework for teacher advocacy, she identifies five disruptor archetypes (the collaborator, the mediator, the rebel rouser, the cheer leader, and the poet) and illustrates the kind of advocacy work each archetype may engage in through a collection of powerful case studies. She notes:

> *Since the Monolingual Bias isn't going anywhere anytime soon, anchored in a country that has an uncomfortable relationship with colonialism—steeped in racial, cultural, and dare I add, linguistic hierarchies of power—then we need actionable and sustainable strategies to build a more just and equitable world for our MLLs.*
>
> (Ardell, 2025, p. 13)

Intersectionality

Kimberlé Crenshaw (1989) coined the term *intersectionality* to explain oppression that results from the convergence of race- and gender-based prejudice, initially to explain the discriminatory practices black women experienced. Since its original inception, the concept of intersectionality has been widely used in education and sociology and it has been helpful to define multiple identities or representations, often steeped in inequalities. "Intersectionality emphasizes that different dimensions of identity are not isolated from one another; instead, they intertwine and overlap in intricate ways, resulting in distinct advantages or disadvantages, benefits or harms" (Samie, 2025, para. 5). A close examination of multilingual learners' demographic and background information is likely to reveal that many multilingual learners are at the intersection of many different identity markers, most notably, a significant number of them are students of color and a considerable portion of them come from low-income households, they are immigrants or children of immigrants.

More specifically, it is important to look out for and identify any forms of linguistic racism (linguicism), which refers to prejudice and discrimination based on someone's language background, language use, or linguistic heritage. In addition, in numerous schools, multilingual learners are overrepresented in special education programs as well, thus making their intersectional learner portraits even more complex. Patricia Martínez-Álvarez (2022) raises a concern that "schools have failed to understand the complexities of children with multiple potential learning identities or the forms of oppression they experience" (pp. 3–4), which may lead to a disproportionate number of students becoming marginalized, misunderstood, and underserved.

Notable Research

Maria Cioè-Peña (2017) identifies a troubling phenomenon for dually identified multilingual learners that she refers to as the intersectional gap, meaning the lack of "truly inclusive spaces for children who have more than one factor affecting their academic development (p. 913).

April Baker-Bell (2020) defines linguistic justice as "an antiracist approach to language and literacy education" (p. 7) and offers a new framework that she refers to as Antiracist Black Language Pedagogy, connecting linguistic, cultural, and racial justice. Baker-Bell argues:

> *Linguistic hierarchies and racial hierarchies are interconnected. That is, people's language experiences are not separate from their racial experiences. Indeed, the way a Black child's language is devalued in school reflects how Black lives are devalued in the world. Similarly, the way a white child's language is privileged and deemed the norm in schools is directly connected to the invisible ways that white culture is deemed normal, neutral, and superior in the world.*
>
> (Baker-Bell, 2020, p. 2)

Nelson Flores and Jonathan Rosa (2015) introduce a raciolinguistic perspective to language pedagogy and caution that simply teaching language-minoritized students to use standard (or appropriate) English is likely to fail due to the racial hierarchy that is inherent in how non-white language use is viewed as deficient and marginalized. Their call to action is to understand how language is tied to race, power and colonial history and destigmatize and demarginalize linguistic diversity.

Pedagogical Injustice

Also referred to as cognitive injustice, pedagogical injustice originates from the daily instructional experiences that disadvantage multilingual learners. As Jeff Zwiers (2024) so powerfully states, "the current model of learning, which is grounded in the accumulation of a set of facts and skills, ignores and devalues the many assets that multilingual students bring with them to the learning table" (p. 1). Languages and multilingual competencies are so much more than tools to communicate, they also serve as essential resources for generating and structuring new understanding.

If students' full linguistic repertoires are not utilized, their academic, social-emotional, and socio-cultural development may be negatively impacted.

Inadequacy of Assessment Tools and Discriminatory Assessment Practices

Home language surveys and initial screening tools are used with high frequency across schools and districts, and they are universally deemed helpful in determining multilingual learners' English proficiency levels and eligibility for language support programs. Most other assessment tools, especially standardized achievement tests and placement tests are normed on English speakers, do not easily distinguish between content knowledge and English language proficiency, carry complex cultural biases reflecting White middle-class values, with valid and reliable versions of these assessments rarely available in multiple languages (Bennett, 2023). Even when more accessible, multilingual, multimodal, or digitally scaffolded assessment tools are available, numerous challenges remain resulting in inequities: access to or implementation of such assessments may be inconsistent across programs, schools, or districts; educators may not be prepared to use and interpret such assessments; translated versions of assessments are rarely equivalent; as well as multilingual learners may have experienced language loss or do not have comparable biliteracy skills.

Program Placement and Student Segregation

Depending on the local context, multilingual learners eligible for language support services may be placed in English only or bilingual programs. This subgroup of students is among those most likely to experience, district-, school-, and classroom-level segregation. Within a district, only designated schools offer certain programs, so students are bused from their neighborhood; within a school, multilingual students may be tracked, and newcomer programs may keep students in segregated classrooms away from English-speaking peers for years; and within the classroom, grouping strategies may isolate same language-speakers from their peers.

One additional troubling area is the overall disparity between multilingual learners' and their English-speaking counterparts' representation in gifted and talented programs, partially due to inadequate assessments, continued segregation of students, and limited teacher training in the area. Allison List and Cass Dykeman (2021) note that only 1–4% of multilingual learners are typically identified to be gifted, when the overall student ratio is up to 10% so disproportional representation is found across the 50 states.

Tapestry of Voices

Deborah Short, founder and director of Academic Language Research & Training, former division director at the Center for Applied Linguistics (CAL), recommends a range of approaches to redressing inequities for multilingual learners, most of which are directly connected to the challenges and opportunities discussed in this chapter so far as well as later herein.

- ★ *Showcase what students and their families know via funds of knowledge activities.*
- ★ *Celebrate academic and extracurricular successes of bilingual/multilingual students.*
- ★ *Promote the Seal of Biliteracy.*
- ★ *Collect and analyze data by language and ethnic group in several areas, such as disciplinary actions, access to advanced coursework, participation in gifted and talented programs and if percentages are low (for ex. are below the total percentage of that group in the school system), take action to make changes.*
- ★ *Offer asset-based professional development for teachers, administrators, counselors, including basic Second Language Acquisition (SLA) research and practical techniques for working with multilingual learners and their families.*

Pause for a Moment

What examples of monolingual bias have you uncovered? What are most readily noticeable and what are harder to identify?
Why is intersectionality such a complex phenomenon when it comes to multilingual learners?
What pedagogical and assessment practices in your context yield the most accurate and useful data regarding multilingual learners? Which ones tend to be the least reliable and most biased? What can be done about it?
What programs are offered to support multilingual learners? What programs are not offered, but could be and should be available?

Long-Term Efforts to Redress Multilingual Injustices

Long-term efforts may vary greatly from school to school, district to district based on what you uncovered. In this section, my goal is to offer some essential cross-cutting responses to multilingual injustices, which must start with what impacts students every day: Policies and practices related to curriculum, instruction, and assessment are interconnected components of our daily work with students. The most fundamental definitions of these concepts reveal that curriculum is what we teach, instruction refers to how we teach the curriculum, and assessment helps us (both teachers and students) find out what has been learned through curriculum and instruction. The key challenges I invite you to face with me are (a) identifying ways to redress multilingual inequities across the three dimensions of curriculum, instruction and assessment and (b) changing the institutional beliefs, policies and practices that present a barrier to doing so.

"All teachers are language teachers!"

"All teachers are literacy teachers!"

"All teachers are teachers of multilingual learners!"

How can these simple slogans or pronouncements be enacted with a deep, long-term commitment with an anti-discriminatory stance, through *deliberate daily actions* (Safir & Dugan, 2021)? I plan to guide you through an exploration of redressing multilingual inequities in the contexts of curriculum, instruction and assessment and by highlighting the importance of ongoing professional learning related to multilingualism.

Tapestry of Voices

Merica Clinkenbeard, Director, English Language Development, Springfield Public Schools, Missouri believes that multilingual justice requires more than good intentions and emphasizes how curricular and instructional choices play an important role.

> *As a program leader, I focus on aligning curriculum, instruction, and professional learning, so language development is not left to chance. Equity work for multilingual learners' lives in the daily decisions we make, especially when we resist deficit explanations and examine the structures that surround students. Sustaining equity means staying committed to this work even when it challenges comfortable or long held practices.*

Similarly, Justin Zhang, international educator and university professor, Namseoul University, South Korea, recognizes how complex multilingual justice and injustice are and emphasizes the importance of curricular, instructional, and assessment practices to ensure equitable learning experiences for multilingual learners.

> *Multilingual injustice often manifests subtly—through curriculum choices, assessment practices, or even classroom interactions that privilege one language over others (i.e., English in most international school settings). It's important to recognize that when students' languages are ignored or devalued, we risk undermining their confidence, engagement, and academic potential. On the other hand, multilingual justice is not just about allowing students to use their home languages; it's about valuing those languages as assets and integrating them*

> *meaningfully into learning. It means designing policies and practices that affirm linguistic diversity as a strength, not a barrier, and giving every learner the opportunity to see themselves reflected in the curriculum.*

Let's start with some ready-to go, easy-to-implement strategies to bring curriculum, instruction, and assessment together. See Table 4.2 for a short list of practices arranged according to these three pedagogical dimensions to redress inequities. Feel free to add further examples of how curricular, instructional and assessment choices create more equitable learning opportunities for multilingual learners. Table 4.2 is merely the springboard; next I will take you on a deeper exploration.

Table 4.2 Practical strategies for linguistically responsive and sustaining practices.

Dimensions	Select linguistically responsive and sustaining strategies
Curriculum	• Augment the curriculum with bilingual or translated resources • Connect students' cultural and linguistic identities and experiences to units or lessons • • • •
Instruction	• Provide multiple access points, including multilingual and multimodal representations • Utilize bilingual peer bridges • Invite translanguaging practices • • •
Assessment	• Encourage bilingual responses to assessment tasks • Make multilingual glossaries and digital scaffolds available • Invite multilingual and multimodal student responses and representations • • •

Curriculum

A curriculum is designed to anchor all the instructional choices and assessment practices teachers make and in which students engage. Curriculum may be defined as a road map, as a scope and sequence document, as a tool to show how conceptual development in a particular subject matter may be achieved, and more. A leading curriculum expert, William Pinar (2004) noted that "the school curriculum communicates what we choose to remember about our past, what we believe about our present, and what we hope for the future" (p. 20). Twenty years later, it still seems to ring true … with some caveats. More recently, Pinar (2023) reminds us that curriculum can never be anything static, not just a list of topics to cover, not merely a scope and sequence no matter how carefully crafted and aligned to standards. It should not even be perceived as a noun.

The Latin root is *currere*, which is an infinitive form of a verb, and it means "to run" or "to move along swiftly." He conceptualizes teachers' and students' experiences with the curriculum as an opportunity for self-formation through a powerful dialogic encounter.

So, let's talk and discuss equity in the curriculum for multilingual learners:

- Who determines what we are supposed to remember about our past?
- Who chooses what we are to believe about our present?
- Who shapes our hope for the future?
- Whose past, present, and future are being considered, valued, and honored?
- And how do languages and cultures fit into the past, present, and future considerations and curriculum decisions?

I have visited lots of districts and schools across the United States and internationally in the past two decades while researching or supporting multilingual professional learning. In addition to the open-minded, equity-oriented, affirming, and uplifting conversations, I have heard a fair share of pushbacks and excuses; reasons and arguments, apologies and fully polished rationalizations for why it is ***not*** doable, possible, feasible, allowable, manageable, workable and achievable to touch the curriculum in any substantial way in support of multilingual learners.

Which of the following *Yes, buts* … have you heard? (Or perhaps you have even spoken some of these before your commitment to multilingual equity work?)

- Yes, but the curriculum is mandated by the district, and we are expected to implement it with fidelity.
- Yes, but we have to cover the curriculum and don't have time for anything extra!

- Yes, but the other students get slowed down by differentiating the curriculum for multilingual learners.
- Yes, but when my parents came to this country, they had to learn English to survive!
- Yes, but it is not my job, I am the _____ [math/science/social studies, etc.] teacher!
- Yes, but we must get students prepared for the upcoming assessment.

You can add a dozen more, I am sure! Which of them have you discussed with your colleagues with a sincere effort to recast them as a possibility for curriculum innovation and not a problem? Which of them have you responded to both in the shorter term and in the longer term to redress inequities?

Tapestry of Voices

Ching-Ching Lin, co-author of *Centering Multilingual Learners in School Curriculum through Community Asset Mapping: A Practical Guide for Teachers*, highlights the importance of supporting student agency and normalizing multilingualism rather than treating it as an exception in the curriculum. She suggests achieving it

> *by overhauling the school curriculum so that it not only reflects diverse perspectives beyond token representation, but also actively empowers students to reshape and reimagine the curriculum itself. This means valuing students' linguistic and cultural assets, involving them as co-creators of knowledge, and positioning their voices at the center of curricular decision-making.*

When educators commit to developing and implementing culturally and linguistically responsive and sustaining curricula, they do the following:

- Make meaningful connections to students' languages, as well as cultural and linguistic identities and lived experiences.
- Prioritize inductive approaches to learning—centering students' inquiry, experiential and cultural knowledge while maintaining rigor and engagement.
- Disrupt the monolingual, monocultural, Eurocentric focus and include diverse literatures, histories, and cultural accomplishments that reflect the students' and the larger cultural communities' backgrounds.
- Select High Quality Instructional Materials (HQIM) in multiple languages and multiple modalities including traditional text-based and digital resources.
- Include student voice and choice.

When the curriculum honors multilingualism and centers multilingual learners, students:

- Develop a deeper understanding of the content by making frequent metacognitive and metalinguistic connections.
- Have full access to the core curriculum through multilingual and multimodal resources.
- Apply or further develop language and literacy competencies in their home languages or heritage languages with enthusiasm.
- Develop a positive self-image and self-efficacy for success.
- Gain confidence in contributing to the classroom community.

Notable Research

Over two decades ago, Grant Wiggins and Jay McTighe noted that teachers have an important, active role in creating curricula for their students:

> *Teachers are designers. An essential act of our profession is the crafting of our curriculum and learning experiences to meet specific purposes. We are also designers of assessments to diagnose student needs to guide our teaching and to enable us, our students, and others (parents and administrators) to determine whether we have achieved our goals.*
>
> (Wiggins & McTighe, 2005, p. 13)

More recently, George C. Bunch and Aída Walqui (2025) also emphasized how critical it is for teachers to engage in designing curricula: "Classroom teachers are the most important curriculum developers, both in terms of creating their own materials and adapting those created by others" (p. 6), yet they also acknowledge that most educators have never been asked to participate in curriculum design with multilingual learners in mind.

Teachers have the power and the responsibility to approach all curriculum work—developing, mapping and aligning—as well as unit and lesson planning with multilingual learners in mind: not as an afterthought but placing multilingualism as a universal value and asset. Curriculum should never be scripted, especially for multilingual learners whose academic, linguistic, and socioemotional development is dynamic and multifaceted! It is important to keep in mind the difference between and among the Intended (Planned) vs. Taught (Enacted) vs. Learned Curriculum when multilingualism is moved from the margins to the center and to shift the questions from simply determining whether multilingualism or a token representation of it is present to how it is prioritized.

- The **intended or planned curriculum** can be found in curriculum guides or scope and sequence documents, unit plans and lesson plans.
  - *How are resources integrated in multiple languages?*
  - *How are multilingual learners' experiences reflected?*
  - *How are multilingual learners' perspectives valued?*
- The **enacted or taught curriculum** refers to the sequence of actual instructional tasks educators implement during the lessons, and teachers and students collaboratively shape into meaningful learning experiences.
  - *How are multiple languages used meaningfully and equitably?*
  - *How do multilingual learners show evidence of learning?*
  - *How do multilingual learners see their cultural and linguistic funds of knowledge and funds of identity?*
- The **learned curriculum** refers to what the students were able to access and develop mastery of during the implementation of the curriculum as evidenced by a range of assessment tools and measures.
  - *How do multilingual learners have equitable access to all learning opportunities?*
  - *How do multilingual learners show their insights and perspectives?*
  - *How do multilingual learners demonstrate their learning and mastery in multiple languages or the language of their choice?*

There are additional challenges multilingual learners face related to curricula. For examples, the **hidden curriculum** (what is not explicitly stated in textbooks and other instructional materials, but implicitly communicated through behaviors and attitudes) may be confusing or outright discriminatory for many students. The **null curriculum** may be even more concerning, since it refers to what is left out of the curriculum intentionally or unintentionally, so students do not have the opportunity to learn.

Pause for a Moment

What curriculum decisions need to be made in your context to be fully inclusive of multilingual learners?

What elements of the existing curricula need to be retained or removed, what needs to be added or revised?

How can you best ensure multilingual justice within the framework of local and state standards?

Instruction

Multilingual justice in the classroom does not mean that everyone must become bilingual or multilingual, although wouldn't that be an amazing feat? Multilingual equity in the instructional context means ensuring that all teaching practices and learning activities are fully available to all students, including multilingual learners regardless of their English language proficiency levels. Access to learning and participating in education is not just a language right, it is a human right. An on-going commitment that instructional practices are equitable is a nonnegotiable aspect of this work, so "every child receives whatever she/he/they need to develop to her/his/their full academic and social potential and to thrive, every day" (Aguilar, 2021, p. 6). For our purposes, let's add one more powerful dimension, and ensure that every child can also develop to their full linguistic potential and thrive while doing so! The tool in the textbox may be used both to self-assess and plan instruction in support of multilingual learners. As before, I invite you to augment this checklist in collaboration with your colleagues to develop shared ownership and long-term commitment to linguistically responsive and sustaining instruction.

Self-Assessment and Planning Checklist

Culturally and linguistically responsive and sustaining instructional practices include:

- ☐ Language-rich, language-affirming classroom and school environments that make multilingualism the norm visible to and appreciated by all.
- ☐ An abundance of experiential, hands-on learning activities that invite students to process learning and to contribute to the classroom experiences in the language and language modality of their preference.
- ☐ "Choice and voice" that lead to student ownership of learning activities and multilingual modes of communication.
- ☐ Opportunities for student self-reflection and goal-setting.
- ☐ Varied, flexible grouping configurations that include same-language and different language partners.
- ☐ Meta-awareness and meta-skill development that includes the following three areas: Metacognitive skills (thinking about thinking), metalinguistic skills (thinking about language), and metacultural skills (thinking about one's own and others' cultural identities and cultural behaviors).

Add more from your own context:

- ☐ ____________________
- ☐ ____________________
- ☐ ____________________
- ☐ ____________________

Scaffolding Instruction

Scaffolding is frequently associated with instructional practices or in the moment supports offered as needed. Aída Walqui and Leo van Lier (2010) call scaffolding in support of multilingual learners the *pedagogy of promise*. They recommend that pedagogical scaffolds "should be constantly changed, dismantled, extended, and adapted in accordance with the needs" of the students (p. 24) and, as such, they can fulfill the promise of amplifying (making it more visible and accessible), rather than simplifying the curriculum. To do this work systematically, we must engage in macro-scaffolding at the unit level, meso-scaffolding at the lesson level, and micro-scaffolding in response to individual needs that may emerge during a particular learning task.

Recently, my colleagues and I have mapped out nine dimensions of scaffolding (Honigsfeld & Dove, 2022; Dove et al., 2026). See Table 4.3 for a summary chart for the name and a brief description of each dimension and a blank column left open for you and your team to engage in a joint exploration of these dimensions and to gather examples from your own context. Ongoing professional learning around ensuring multilingual learner success in a comprehensive way is necessary to redress inequities in the classroom.

One critical aspect of multilingual equity and justice is connected to student engagement and participation in every aspect of instruction. When students feel undervalued and silenced in classrooms where only appropriate monolingual language use is the norm (Flores & Rosa, 2015), their linguistic capacities will not grow in any language.

Translanguaging as a Pedagogy of Multilingual Justice

For multilingual learners, languages and language practices should never be forcefully and artificially separated. Instead, I urge you to embrace the concept of the *corriente*, or river current, of multilingual language use and visualize how languages flow freely into each other (Maldonado Rodríguez & Krause, 2020). According to one of the most frequently quoted definitions of translanguaging, it is a process in which, "bilingual speakers select meaning-making features [from multiple languages] and freely combine them to potentialize meaning-making, cognitive engagement, creativity, and criticality" (García & Wei, 2014, p. 42). Translanguaging is not the same as translating, neither is it the same as code-switching, so let's take a closer look to ensure clarity and consistency how we define and enact this approach for lasting impact on policy and practice.

In bilingual education programs, especially the dual language context, translanguaging has taken hold over the years, no longer forcing one language on the students during designated class periods, or reminding students to stick to one language in their communicative efforts. However, many monolingual teachers in predominantly English-speaking classroom contexts

Table 4.3 Multidimensional scaffolding for multilingual learners.

Scaffolding approach	Brief description of each approach	Examples from own practice
Instructional	Guiding students through the entire learning experience through strategic lesson planning and delivery	
Linguistic	Supporting language and literacy development at the word, sentence, and discourse dimensions	
Multimodal	Encouraging expressive (speaking, writing, visually representing) and interpretive (listening, reading, viewing) modes of language	
Multisensory	Arranging auditory, visual, tactile, and kinesthetic experiences	
Graphic	Providing schematic or visual representations	
Digital	Applying technology-based tools and techniques	
Interactive/ collaborative	Ensuring active participation, engaged communication, and joint task completion	
Social-emotional	Offering affective supports and ensuring relationship building	
Environmental	Creating a physical and virtual learning context most conducive to learning	

Source: adapted from Honigsfeld & Dove (2022, p. 206)

may wonder, why does this apply to me? How would I even start implementing it in my classroom?

The use of multilingual learners' full linguistic repertoires optimizes all their learning experiences as students tap into all the linguistic systems available to them at the same time. Metaphorically speaking, Nelson Flores (2020) reminds us that multilingual learners build their lives on their *full language architecture,* so our responsibility is to honor that and capitalize on their languages as an essential dimension of the funds of knowledge and funds of identity they bring to school with them (Esteban-Guitart & Moll, 2014; Gonzalez et al., 2005). As they construct their linguistic and cultural identities, all languages (both the *named,* official languages such as English, Spanish, Urdu, etc.) as well as their authentic communicative practices and linguistic resources—often referred to as *unnamed*—must be available to them.

You might wonder why translanguaging matters so much for multilingual justice? Isn't it an individual linguistic strategy students engage in if they choose to do so? Translanguaging has also been recognized as part of a systemic approach to cultural inclusionary practices (Xu & Valdez, 2023) as well as a continuum to ensure educational equity by listening to, challenging and flowing with the *corriente* of translanguaging (Parra & Proctor, 2022). Melissa Gibson (2024) redefines viewing language and multilingualism in the context of teaching social studies and suggests that translanguaging as multilingual learners' legitimate "language practice can be the very embodiment of students' civic identities" (p. 19). There is an ever-expanding body of research and practical recommendations based on translanguaging, but you might wonder what translanguaging pedagogy looks like in the classroom and how to make sure it becomes the norm across all program models, grade levels, and subject matter classes. The following ideas constitute a list of possibilities. Since the goal is to honor students' fluid, dynamic multilingual language practices and to capitalize on students' and teachers' creativity and authenticity with language use, continue the list with more examples from your own classroom or from others you might visit across your school or district.

Start here with translanguaging pedagogy:

- ◆ Students discuss an instructional task in small group configurations using all their communicative resources.
- ◆ Students reflect on their own work and share their reflections with a classmate.
- ◆ Students use bilingual dictionaries and discuss concepts with same-language partners in the languages of their choice.

- Students access concepts and skills in their chosen language first (watch a video, read a short text, interview their family or community members).
- Students use both languages in their speech and writing to uncover meaning.
- Students share what they have discovered about how languages work by virtue of tapping into their multilingual and multimodal communicative choices (for example, they contribute to a multilingual word wall, or identify Latin and Greek roots and cognates across languages they are familiar with).
- Students' metalinguistic insights across languages.

Add examples from your own context:

-
-
-
-
-

Move to deeper translanguaging practices:

- Students preview the new lesson in their primary language—participate in the target lesson in English and review the concepts or skills in their primary language again.
- Students research a topic online and use both digital and print-based resources in the language of their choice, summarize their understanding and generate new ideas in more than one language.
- Students draft in one language, discuss and peer edit using both classmates' chosen language practices, and produce the final response in English.
- Students complete a task and display their new learning using all the languages available to them.
- Teachers not only accept or invite translanguaging practices, but model them for the students.
- Students have opportunities to research literature highlighting translanguaging.

Add examples from your own context:

◆

◆

◆

◆

◆

> **Pause for a Moment**
>
> What instructional decisions need to be made in your context to be fully inclusive of multilingual learners?
>
> What pedagogical practices must be replaced versus retained, introduced and cultivated?
>
> How can you best ensure multilingual justice in every classroom, every day?

Assessment

Similar to instructional practices, assessments must also capitalize on students' full linguistic repertoires and invite multimodal and multilingual representations of their learning. Traditional paper and pencil tests, quizzes, or any form of assessment that requires students to recall and produce content only in English will fall short of revealing how much multilingual learners know and can do (Gottlieb, 2021, 2024). Along with many others, I, too, advocate for making project-based, problem-based, and performance-based assessments the go-to approaches for gauging mastery of content learning, as well as monitoring student progress of content, language, and literacy development collaboratively (Gottlieb & Honigsfeld, 2025). This way, you and your team are more likely to stop over relying on the often-incomplete data compiled about multilingual learners from standardized tests; instead, you will begin and continue to focus on gathering data from assessments that give students fair and equitable opportunities to demonstrate their learning. Assessment for multilingual learners is a complex process that should help monitor and accurately document student progress while making intentional use of students' multilingual repertoires.

Tapestry of Voices

Khalil El-Saghir, Multilingual Consultant, Wayne Regional Educational Service Agency, Michigan, urges educators to redefine achievement and fully embrace an asset-based perspective of multilingual learners:

> *Multilingual learners are often treated as if their language practices are barriers to overcome rather than intellectual assets to build upon. In my work, equity begins when systems stop asking how students should adapt to school and start asking how schools must adapt to students. Multilingual justice requires us to redesign policies, assessments, and even definitions of "achievement" so linguistic diversity is recognized as evidence of cognitive strength, not instructional deficit. When systems change, the narrative about multilingual learners changes with them.*

Also from Michigan, Christopher J. Wilinski, Special Education Resource Room Teacher, Hamtramck Public Schools, shares his perspective on fair and meaningful assessments:

> *In my current work with multilingual learners with disabilities, I see how easily language difference is mistaken for deficits, especially when standardized assessments are used to decide who deserves support. As a Polish American, I often imagine what it would feel like to return to Poland and be judged by a standardized language assessment to determine my intelligence, potential, or worthiness of support. That thought guides my work with multilingual learners and students with disabilities, reminding me that language proficiency is not a measure of ability. Multilingual justice, for me, means resisting deficit-based systems and advocating for assessments and practices that honor students' identities, experiences, and humanity."*

Specific strategies to capture multifaceted, meaningful and actionable assessment data as evidence of student learning include:

- Invite students to choose the language(s) and modes of communication that they feel most comfortable and confident in demonstrating their understanding.
- Have students to compile portfolios of their work in any language and collaboratively gauge their progress over time.
- Use rubrics co-constructed with students to assess multilingual learners' oral and written responses, hands-on projects, and experiments, and to offer students feedback.
- Provide students with opportunities for self-assessment, peer-assessment, and assessing their and others' performance in group assignments using multimodal and multilingual tools.

- Include authentic, real-world multilingual communication and language use in assessment tasks such as conducting interviews and completing community-based projects.
- Accept evidence of learning in multiple languages.

Add examples from your own context:

-
-
-
-
-

Margo Gottlieb writes extensively on and advocates for how assessment for multilingual learners can contribute to social justice and equity:

> Multilingual learners deserve relevant and fair assessment that generates useful information for improving teaching and learning in linguistically and culturally sustainable ways. Anything less is not equitable, just or worthwhile. We assert that largely missing has been an educational system that embraces assessment in multiple languages. When multilingual learners show their full linguistic and academic repertoires that are recognized across classrooms, schools and districts, we enhance their opportunities for success in school and beyond.
>
> (Gottlieb, 2022, p. xxvi)

Pause for a Moment

What assessment decisions need to be made in your context to be fully inclusive of multilingual learners?

What assessment practices must be replaced versus retained, introduced and cultivated?

How can you best ensure multilingual justice with assessment?

Tapestry of Voices

Jeff Zwiers, author and former senior researcher at the Stanford Graduate School of Education, has several recommendations to create equity for multilingual learners. Prominent among them are the types of curricular, instructional and assessment choices we make:

1. *Creating, adapting, and using curriculums that value multilingual students' backgrounds, capitals, needs, and languages. It means using teaching practices and choosing content (where possible) that engages students and connects to their background knowledges and experiences. It means not using curriculums and practices that promote accumulation of information and skills for the main purpose of increasing test scores. For example, choosing literature that connects to students' lives.*
2. *Creating and using assessments and assessment practices that connect to students' lives and interests. This includes (rather than or in addition to) using performances and products that motivate students to build up robust disciplinary ideas and then communicate them to real others (e.g., science poster presentations, podcast interviews, business plans, dramatizations, projects, etc.).*
3. *Drastically improving instructional programs and classes that support multilingual students. Providing just enough extra language support in designated ELD classes without sacrificing the time that students spend in history, science, and elective classes. Plus providing in every classroom lots of language-rich classroom activities (with lots of student-student interactions).*

Professional Learning to Redress Multilingual Inequities in Curriculum, Instruction, and Assessment

To achieve much-needed shifts in policies and practices that dismantle multilingual inequities, all educators need equity-oriented professional learning. All means all, so these professional learning opportunities must include administrators at all levels, such as district and school leaders, school board members who often act as local and regional policy-makers, instructional and non-instructional professional staff including paraeducators, who interact with the students during the school day. Building systemic knowledge of multilingualism and multilingual justice and translating that knowledge to policy and practice require institutional commitments. I will revisit professional learning as an equity literacy ability to sustain multilingual justice in Chapter 6. Here, I invite you to learn about District 428's multiyear effort to respond to inequities and to build a more inclusive learning community for multilingual learners.

Spotlight on Multilingual Justice

Val Peña-Hernández is an educational leader and consultant whose work in multilingual education and inclusive systems has been shaped through years of collaboration with district leaders across Illinois. She shares how her professional journey has been deeply influenced by her experiences working alongside AJ Crook in District 428, Illinois.

> I have had the privilege of knowing AJ Crook, District 428's Multilingual Coordinator, through many roles—as my supervisor, instructor, district colleague, and friend. Through each of these lenses, I have witnessed leadership that is not performative, but patient; not reactive, but rooted. Her work has shaped not only a district, but also the way I now understand systems, equity, and what it truly means to lead with purpose.
>
> In the early years of multilingual expansion, District 428, like many districts across the country, was learning how to respond to rapid demographic change. What began as a set of well-intentioned programs gradually became something more: a collective commitment to coherence, to reflection, and to building systems that could grow alongside the students they serve.
>
> This shift did not happen through mandates or quick solutions. It unfolded slowly, through dialogue, professional learning, shared leadership, and a willingness to ask hard questions about access, identity, and belonging. Over time, the district moved from fragmented supports toward a more integrated, research-aligned approach to multilingual education.
>
> One of the clearest expressions of this long journey is the district's dual language pathways. Dual language did not arrive as a single decision or initiative. It emerged through years of groundwork, aligning curriculum, staffing, leadership structures, and instructional practices around the belief that bilingualism is not a barrier, but a strength. Today, these pathways stand as a living reflection of the district's commitment to equity, excellence, and linguistic justice.
>
> As the work deepened, responsibility expanded. Multilingual education became not the charge of one department, but a shared endeavor woven into the fabric of the district. Leaders, teachers, and teams began to see multilingual learners not as exceptions within the system, but as central to its purpose.

What exists now is not the result of a moment, but of a movement, shaped by trust, persistence, and the steady leadership of individuals who believed in what the district could become. Through her long-term commitment to systems-building, AJ Crook has helped shape both the present structures and the future direction of multilingual education in District 428. Together with district leaders, teachers, and teams, she has helped cultivate a shared belief that students deserve learning environments that honor who they are and who they are becoming.

This is the truth of systemic change: it is not loud, fast, or finished. It is quiet, steady, and enduring. It grows through people who choose, again and again, to build something better, together.

Moving Beyond Redressing Multilingual Inequities

To eliminate the root causes of multilingual inequities in the three targeted areas (curriculum, instruction, and assessment) discussed in this chapter and actively move to cultivating multilingual justice and equity, we need ongoing, equity-oriented professional learning. The next two chapters will address how to cultivate and sustain multilingual equity by emphasizing collaboration in and outside the school context and other actionable steps.

End-of-Chapter Reflections

As you finish exploring the third ability of equity literacy, redressing inequities and injustices, reflect on the following:

- ★ What tools and strategies would you use to identify the underlying causes of multilingual inequities and injustices?
- ★ What curricular, instructional and assessment practices may be harmful to multilingual learners' academic, linguistic, and social-emotional development?
- ★ What types of curricular, instructional and assessment decisions need to be made to ensure multilingual equity and justice?

5

How to Cultivate Multilingual Equity and Justice

Have you ever?

Have you ever been weighed down by the lightest question?
Have you ever been swept away by stillness?
Have you ever seen simplicity in the most overwhelming experiences?
Have you ever felt awe by witnessing the most ordinary?

The multilingual experiences in schools are complex and multifaceted without simple formulas or ready-to-go solutions to address deep-rooted problems and daily challenges, biases and prejudices, inequities and injustices that arise along the way. Multilingual learners are as diverse as any other subgroup of students when all identity markers, familial and cultural backgrounds, academic and life experiences are considered. Understanding and honoring such complexities and achieving success with eradicating inequities require hard work and collaboration.

Tapestry of Voices

Pam Schwallier, Director of English Learner & Bilingual Programs in West Ottawa Public Schools, Holland, Michigan, describes the multi-year, intentional work that has taken place in her district:

Serving more than 1,000 multilingual learners across 14 schools in our district, the urgency of realizing multilingual justice is lived daily in

DOI: 10.4324/9781003644071-5

our classrooms and communities. I am guided by the belief, "If not now, when? If not us, who?" While today's educators did not create the systems that have historically marginalized multilingual learners and their families, we are certainly responsible for dismantling them and building equitable systems that honor and serve our students. Through intentional collaboration, the breaking down of silos, and a deliberate shift toward asset-based mindsets, our district has expanded from 12 to 28 full-time ESL teachers in just four years, while 90 educators are currently earning their MA in TESOL through a statewide grant partnership with a local university. This work affirms a powerful truth: when educators act with collective urgency and responsibility, meaningful and lasting change is possible!

Rhonda Hittenberger Ortiz, Missouri English Language Learner (MELL) Instructional Specialist at Missouri State University, Springfield, Missouri affirms that professional learning partnerships foster equitable educational practices for Multilingual Learners:

One of the most pervasive and damaging forms of inequity facing multilingual learners is the belief that "treating all students the same" guarantees fairness. This mindset erases multilingual learners' linguistic, cultural, and academic assets and perpetuates systemic barriers to opportunity. Ensuring equity requires deliberate efforts to center the needs of multilingual learners within cross-curricular conversations. As a regional multilingual learner instructional specialist, I actively partner with experts who support school districts across content areas and student services. I advocate for equity by co-leading professional learning that positions multilingual learners as a shared responsibility—not the work of a single department or specialist. Through collaboration with experts in the fields of special education, school counseling, mathematics, literacy, and new teacher training, we confront deficit-based assumptions, elevate the assets of multilingual learners, and strengthen educators' capacity to implement inclusive, high-impact instructional practices across systems.

So far in this book, I have invited you to look back at such complexities, develop a deep understanding of inequities—to recognize them, to respond to them, and to redress them. All my prior recommendations were aimed at rectifying the harm already done by past actions, existing policies, and prevailing practices. It is time to adjust our perspective! Having background training and experience in yoga and meditation, I often bring a powerful message from these practices to my personal and professional life: Be fully present and bring your awareness to the here and now. Resist distractions and let go of judgment.

You might be thinking that all this works on the yoga mat or in a meditation retreat, but how is it going to advance the multilingual justice we set out to do? I am ready to tackle that, are you? What I am inviting you to do next is consider what has changed in your context as a result of the equity work you have done so far. What works, what is observable, what is presently available, and what must continue to improve this academic year, this month, this week, or even this day. Staying in the present—for the present—may offer much-needed clarity and focus.

As Paul Gorski and Katy Swalwell (2023b) note, "when we actively cultivate equity, we make the equitable decision upfront rather than waiting until damage has been done" (p. 25). I cannot resist this opportunity to examine the etymology of the word *cultivate*. Another Latin root, the original meaning of "cultivare" is tilling or preparing the soil for plants. By the 1700s, the word *cultivate* started to be used more figuratively meaning "to improve, to devote one's attention to" (Etymonline, 2026, para 1). And that is exactly our charge: to continue to improve what we are already doing in support of multilingual learners and to continue to devote our unwavering attention to uplift multilingual equity and justice.

As we explored it in previous chapters, a lot of harm and damage are possible when no intentional focus is given to linguistic diversity, when multilingualism is undervalued, or when multilingual learners are marginalized or excluded from equitable learning opportunities. Any lessons learned must be owned and shared across the school to prevent future repetitions. Past mistakes must be corrected. Future actions must be intentional by building collaborative professional agency and taking collective responsibility.

Tapestry of Voices

Julie Sugarman, Associate Director for K-12 Education Research at MPI's National Center on Immigrant Integration Policy, recognizes that schools and districts might not be in the same place when it comes to equity work, yet she recommends some actionable steps all can engage in on behalf of multilingual learners:

> *Some places across the US urgently need to acknowledge that racism exists at all, and others are ready to do deep anti-bias work. Wherever a school system is on that spectrum, they can make progress toward cultivating multilingual equity by (1) ensuring that individuals with expertise*

in ML education are involved in high-level decision-making at the state, district, and school level; (2) offering continuous professional development on equity (3) establishing clear criteria for defining equitable outcomes; and (4) encouraging regular self-reflection and pair/group debriefing on difficult decisions.

Let's agree

Let's ensure no one has to compromise, hide, or erase their
cultural linguistic heritage or identity.
Let's create learning environments where all language
backgrounds are valued and actively utilized.
Let's empower multilingual learners and their families to fully
participate and thrive in all communities.
Let's continue to learn as educators, leaders, and policymakers
to deeply understand the complexities of multilingualism
Let's remain focused on equity and justice for multilingual learners
so they, too, could realize their full potential
Let's reject deficit-oriented discourse and action that may distract
from or derail our efforts
Let's agree!
Agree?

Cultivating Equity from Multilingual Learners' Arrival to Graduation

The moment a multilingual child arrives until the day they graduate or leave our schools, numerous decisions are made. Many of them happen during instructional time in the classroom, yet even more far-reaching ones outside, in the larger context of the school, district, and community. While cultivating multilingual justice is a must, educators face the challenge of operating within federal and state mandates as well as locally developed district and school policies. What James Crawford (2008) stated close to two decades ago continues to prevail in numerous contexts, "decisions on how to teach English learners are being made not in the classroom, but in legislative chambers and voting booths; not on the basis of educational research data, but on the basis of public opinion, often passionate but rarely informed" (p. 59).

Educational policy decisions have always been political. The legislation of the Bilingual Education Act (BEA) of 1968 was designed to address the perceived verbal deprivation, poverty of experiences, and other supposed language-based and cultural deficiencies in bilingual homes through in-school remediation. The landmark U.S. Supreme Court decision of *Lau v. Nichols* in 1974 stated that "there is no equality of treatment merely by providing the same facilities, textbooks, teachers and curriculum for students who do not understand English effectively." As a result of the 1981 *Castañeda vs. Pickard* case, in order to comply with the Lau decision, schools must serve multilingual learners through programs based on sound educational theory; utilize appropriate resources and personnel to successfully implement the program; and carry out rigorous evaluation that shows the effectiveness of the program.

In the past 50 years, additional federal and state guidelines have been put in place to protect the key rights of English learners/multilingual learners and to determine state-level expectations for language support and accountability measures (often connected to annual assessments).

Tapestry of Voices

Tatyana Kleyn, Professor, Bilingual Education & TESOL Programs, The City College of New York, offers three recommendations to cultivate equity for multilingual learners, including advocacy for students and families:

> *(1) Ensuring that funding remains available for students labeled as ELLs regardless of federal mandates, (2) Developing bilingual programs in middle and high schools with more students new to English at the secondary level, and (3) Connecting language justice to migration justice by creating supports and forging partnerships for immigrant-origin students and families.*

Notable Research

Nelson Flores and Mark Lewis (2022) caution about the continued dichotomies that policies establish among bilingual students (such as English learners or ELs and non-English learners or non-ELs) and suggest "a more general framing of bilingualism in education that breaks away from the remedial orientation of the Bilingual Education Act and subsequent EL policy environment" (p. 14). They also recommend that, as a result, educators could "design differentiated support that benefit[s] all bilingual students without the need to identify their supposed linguistic limitations to justify this support" (p. 14).

Determining who is eligible for what type of services and who benefits from what type of placement continues to be a challenge. I still remember how many years ago, as a new ESL (the title used at the time was English as a Second Language) teacher in the New York City Public Schools in the 1990s, I was told to administer the Language Assessment Battery-Revised (LAB-R) test to all incoming students with Hispanic last names, many of whom were fully proficient in English and Spanish! Some of those students might have had a bad day, others might have been confused by a test question or two and ended up classified in need of ESL services. We have come a long way, but we have to keep improving educational policies and practices with the goal of creating and sustaining multilingual justice!

Lau Plans

Although the federal role in English learner/bilingual education has been significant, there has never been adequate funding nor comprehensive equity-oriented guidance available to support multilingual learners; therefore, the urgency to act locally has never been more important.

One way to achieve a high-impact, systemic approach to cultivating equity for multilingual learners at the school and district levels is to collaboratively create a Lau Plan, review it, and improve it annually.

There are Lau Plan templates available on many state departments of education websites; however, Tamara Eklöf, Rebecca Callahan, and Stephanie Vogel (2025) found that "sound, effective, evidence-based systems and structures" (p. 28) for language support programs may be challenging, especially in low-incidence contexts. The team approached this challenge by creating a comprehensive, free, open-access tool, which is a carefully crafted rubric to both self-assess and guide district and school leadership teams as they create and build the infrastructure necessary for equitable, effective education for multilingual learners.

(You can access the tool here:
www.oakbridgeconsultingllc.com/about-lau-plan-guidance-tool
Included here with permission.)

The tool is aligned to the guidance offered in the English Learner Toolkit (US Department of Education, 2017), and its goal is not only to offer compliance guidelines but help adopt evidence-based practices across the ten dimensions:

1 identification of potential ML-EL students. Subsequent rows and chapters then cover,
2 providing ML-EL identified students with a language assistance/EL program,

3. staffing and supporting an EL program,
4. providing ML-EL identified students with equal access to curricular and extracurricular programs,
5. creating an inclusive environment and avoiding unnecessary segregation of ML-EL identified students,
6. addressing ML-EL identified students with disabilities,
7. serving ML-EL identified students' who opt out of EL programs or services,
8. monitoring and exiting ML-EL identified students from EL programs and services,
9. evaluating EL program effectiveness, and
10. meaningful communication with parents and guardians of ML-EL identified students.

While all these dimensions of cultivating equity for multilingual learners are important, three frequently cited challenges are over-representation, under-representation, and misidentification of multilingual learners in special education programs. To better understand the intersection of language development and multilingual learners' unique learning needs, my colleagues and I have long been advocating for teacher collaboration (Gottlieb & Honigsfeld, 2025; Honigsfeld & Dove, 2026; Honigsfeld & Cohan, 2024). This is especially important during the pre-referral phase and the early stages of identification and student placement in the *least restrictive environment* (LRE). I appreciate how Amanda Kibler (2023) flips the narrative on it and refers to it as the most *expansive learning environment*, where all students enjoy their *rightful presence* (not merely inclusion) and receive *educational dignity* (not merely supports). Language is powerful! To initiate and sustain change in support of multilingual learners, what we say and advocate for, as well as how we say it and advocate for it also matters!

When multiple perspectives are sought from different educators, psychologists, speech pathologists, caregivers, and others interacting with the student, a more accurate and comprehensive assessment of a student's cultural, academic, linguistic, and other assets and needs is possible.

- Without a focus on educational equity, it is easy to overlook students' multiple learning identities.
- Without educators taking a collaborative approach and without combining their expertise, it is harder to understand students' complex needs as well as the most effective pathways to their success.
- Without the leadership's commitment to all of this to happen, systemic change for multilingual learners will not occur.

Since Lau Plans are revised annually, they present an ongoing opportunity to closely examine every key element of the plan and to intentionally cultivate equity through collaborative work. Data from multilingual learning walks and multilingual equity audits (as suggested in Chapter 4) will be instrumental in informing many details in the plan. When educators center multilingualism and multilingual learners rather than continue to marginalize them, everyone benefits. When educators actively seek opportunities to better understand how equity improves education for multilingual learners, everyone benefits.

Pause for a Moment

Lau Plans focus on multilingual learners who are eligible for language support programs.

What are some additional ways that all multilingual learners' complex language, literacy, academic and social emotional development may be supported in equitable and just ways?

How can your district's Lau Plan become more than a digital file?

Spotlight on Multilingual Justice

Kelly Cray, Cultural and Language Support educator at Burr and Burton Academy, Manchester Center, VT, shares her and her school's efforts to make English no longer the unquestioned center of school life:

> The fourth ability of equity literacy is active cultivation, which describes the work of going beyond noticing and responding to inequities that are part of the fabric of everyday life. The systems and institutions are built around the dominant language, culture, or communication preferences. For me, developing an equity lens took the willingness to sit with hard truths and interrupt my own autopilot. It was unsettling, then, and it is still unsettling now. I sit with it anyway.
>
> Once you see the inequities, you cannot look away. It is in policies, interactions, expectations, and routines; it is not situational, it lives in our structures. Seeing the world clearly, with its disparities exposed permanently, reshapes how a leader sees their role.
>
> Cultivating equity moves us into institutional habit. This is not a strategic plan for equity initiatives, but a system intentionally built to reduce harm and support multilingualism from the outset. This looks like creating psychological safety, recognizing linguistic assets, and honoring agency. To weave language justice into a school's culture, rituals, and identity also means confronting the relationship between English and power in the face of discomfort and resistance.

In my own practice, building a durable system is a deliberate and strategic act that begins with Bolman and Deal's (2021) Four Frames of Leadership. Their framework reminds us that schools are systems, human communities, political arenas, and symbolic cultures all at once. The most coherent, responsive, and increasingly automatic work means attending to all the frames at once, which is what I mapped out in Table 5.1. Schools are active systems that cannot be shut down for transformation, so changes need to be responsive, operate at multiple levels simultaneously, and occur in the course of regular business.

Table 5.1 The Four Frames of Leadership through a multilingual justice lens.

Leadership frame	Core	What it looks like through a multilingual justice lens
Structural	Policies, schedules, SOPs, organizational design	Building translation timelines into workflows Designing inclusive placement processes (not solely around English proficiency) Hiring practices reward multilingualism Implementing equitable and concrete multilingual grading policies
Human resources	People, relationships, capacity, professional identity	Coaching teachers to reduce microaggressions Offering professional development that honors multilingualism Supporting multilingual staff rather than using them as unpaid translators
Political	Power, coalitions, competing interests, scarce resources	Protecting MLs from deficit-based narratives Anticipating what adult fears will manifest, and addressing them directly Using data and stories to shift allegiance
Symbolic	Culture, rituals, stories, symbols, meaning-making	Using multilingual signage Normalizing home languages as intellectual Celebrating linguistic identity Publicly recognizing bilingual assets

Since I took over the EL teaching and coordination responsibilities at my school approximately seven years ago, I am very proud of the shifts we have made, but equity work remains an ongoing process. I started with the LAU plan and did not redraft it all in the first year; instead, I embraced the slow pivot. I realized that some of what I saw as faults in the system, others saw as points of pride. They believed they knew their community well enough to anticipate every need, and this knowledge was part of their professional identity. I had to pull data to show that students were waiting too long for support because many families hid their multilingual identities and worked very hard to demonstrate their English proficiency. This was not one conversation, but many over the years, until we reached a place I had been hoping for. I needed to make sure members of my school community were ready to walk with me and put in stopgap measures to ensure students got what they needed in the meantime.

There was fear. If students could speak to each other in a language staff and faculty did not know, then some control would be lost. Naming this came from a place of vulnerability and only surfaced when I suspected it might be driving hesitation and asked directly. I began bringing students with me to share their hopes and dreams with their teachers, as we worked out how to support them in learning AP Chemistry alongside English. Teachers were nervous about the responsibility of teaching complex material across a language barrier, as though willingly taking it on shifted the "fault" from the student to themselves.

Embracing the language-justice mindset was difficult at first, but then it felt like magic. When the theme for my first school year was announced—"Kaizen: Change for Good"—it became my opening to link appreciation for language to our school identity. From there, we were able to redefine our annual language testing into a week-long celebration of multilingualism. Others began speaking more openly about their multilingual identities. We added the Seal of Biliteracy program. Now we see multilingualism everywhere, from interviews with alumni in our biannual magazine to mixed-language stage productions.

Still, we are not finished. The next step is to invite more of our monolingual students to understand and embrace this part of our campus, even if they speak only one language and do not feel closely connected to other cultures. This is the demographic that is most missing, and where many of the microaggressions seem to originate. We plan to make the year-end expo fully multilingual and accessible to encourage broader community mixing. Our hope is that students will value the partnerships required to translate their work into other languages so that all people can read it, and that this pride will nurture deeper respect.

Pause for a Moment

What in this Spotlight story spoke to you the most?
How does Table 5.1 support your understanding of leadership support for multilingual justice?

Program Models

Multilingual learners who are also identified as English learners are entitled to receive language support. Over the past few decades, we have seen a slow but steady move away from isolated, skills-based instructional models to more integrated approaches that address age- and grade-appropriate learning opportunities, general education content area standards, disciplinary literacy, and social-emotional development. This paradigm shift may directly be connected to moving away from a deficit-oriented perspective and a monolingual, English-only approach to valuing students' multilingual identities and rich linguistic assets. There are numerous program models that support students' language and literacy development, with different levels of home language or multilingual support.

Table 5.2 contains a summary of the major programs, a brief description and overarching goals of each program, and the primary student groups(s) who participate in them. I invite you to look for a pattern of student groups associated with each program and pay close attention to where and how multilingualism may be or could be valued more. Even if not all of these program models are familiar to you or available in your district or school, consider how equity and multilingual justice may be connected to each.

Pause for a Moment

Which of these program models are currently offered in your context?
How equitable are they in serving multilingual learners?
Which program models are possibly being phased in or even phased out in your district and school?
What changes would you like to see to program models?
What are the barriers to make any program-based experiences more equitable for all?

Table 5.2 Program models supporting language and literacy development.

Programs	Equity challenges and opportunities	Program goals	Target student population
Stand-alone English language development programs	Classes may be organized according to students' levels of English language proficiency and/or grade levels Instruction may or may not focus on or align academic content to students' grade level curricula	To develop English language proficiency	Multilingual learners designated as English learners
Integrated ELD programs	Student populations and student support services are integrated. Classes may be co-taught or instructed by a dually certified/endorsed teacher of ELD and ELA	To develop English language proficiency while also learning grade-level content	Multilingual learners designated as English learners
Transitional bilingual education (TBE) programs	Student population is segregated (only students who speak the same primary language are placed in the same class) TBE facilitates the transition to an all-English, monolingual instructional program, both in early and late exit structures	To develop academic skills in students' primary language while developing language, literacy, and academic competence in English	Multilingual learners designated as English learners
Two-way dual language programs	Students are provided literacy and content instruction through two languages while also developing bilingualism and biliteracy, grade-level academic achievement, and sociocultural competence	To develop grade-level academic skills, biliteracy, and sociocultural competence through two languages	All students [close to equal numbers of students who are monolingual/dominant in either of the program languages]

One-way dual language programs	Students from the same primary or home language/background have the opportunity to be bilingual or multilingual, while maximizing the number of Els to participate in the program as a matter of equity and access to grade-level content/curriculum	To develop grade-level, academic skills, biliteracy, and sociocultural competence through two languages	Linguistically homogeneous groups of students
Heritage language programs	Heritage programs are any language development program designed to address the needs of heritage language learners/speakers at any level or setting, including community-based, K-12, and higher education. These programs allow learners to build/strengthen skills and make various connections they may have in their cultural and linguistic heritages.	To develop language and academic skills in the home/heritage language	Heritage language speakers [those with some language skills and/or a cultural connection to that language through family, community, or country of origin, including Indigenous peoples]
World language immersion programs	Predominantly elementary/K-8 and content-based classes	To acquire language and literacy skills in the target language (other than English)	All students
World language programs	Predominantly secondary classes are formed for language acquisition purposes	To acquire foundational language and literacy skills in the target language	All students

Source: adapted from Lachance & Honigsfeld (2023, pp. 6–7)

Dual Language Education

Dual Language Education program models are uniquely positioned to honor and sustain students' home languages, while also ensuring full access to the grade-level core content and fostering language and literacy development in two linguistic contexts. According to the *Guiding Principles of Dual Language Education*:

> *dual language refers to any program that provides literacy and content instruction to all students through two languages and that promotes bilingualism and biliteracy, grade-level academic achievement, and sociocultural competence—a term encompassing identity development, cross-cultural competence, and multicultural appreciation—for all students. Dual language programs can be either one-way or two-way depending on the student population.*
>
> (Howard et al., 2018, p. 3)

Also referred to as Dual Language Bilingual Education (DLBE) programs, they represent high-impact approaches that offer a systemic way to embed multilingual justice into instruction (Cervantes-Soon et al., 2017; Freire et al., 2024; Palmer et al., 2019b). Decades of research and successful implementation have revealed four pillars of effective dual language programs:

1. ***Bilingualism and biliteracy***—to develop oracy and literacy in the two program languages.
2. ***Grade-level academic achievement***—to achieve grade-level academic attainment in both program languages by meticulously aligning language development in two languages with content learning.
3. ***Sociocultural competence***—to honor and affirm students' cultural backgrounds, to positively shape their multilingual identities, and to interact with others in a manner that respects their multidimensional identities and language use.
4. ***Critical consciousness***—to recognize inequities in dual language programming and to center the voices and experiences of traditionally marginalized students.

I must acknowledge that dual language programs are not without challenges when it comes to equity. A growing number of studies and podcasts have documented an alarming trend they refer to as gentrification of dual language programs. It describes the process of targeting and enrolling students with White middle class or affluent family backgrounds while leaving multilingual learners also classified as English learners behind (Cervantes-Soon et al., 2021; Roda & Menken, 2024). Research by Kate Menken and colleagues (2023) examined the impact of school choice and found that "an influx of more privileged students can push out and/or marginalize the very students for whom DLBE programs were developed" (p. 449). Possible solutions include clarifying and maintaining a vision of providing "socially transformative, culturally affirming education" (Bernstein et al., 2024, p. 272) as well as creating programs and policies that center previously marginalized communities.

Tapestry of Voices

Cristina Sánchez-López, Co-President of Paridad Education Consulting, Chicago, Illinois, has five recommendations to actively cultivate equity in multilingual education, one of which is to enhance access to dual language and bilingual learning opportunities for all K-12 students.

1. *Adopt language-friendly policies at the district level (https://languagefriendlyschool.org).*
2. *Incorporate the topic of linguistic injustice in US history for educators in undergraduate and graduate courses.*
3. *Design and implement professional learning on how to support bilingualism in multilingual settings.*
4. *Implement dual language projects and approaches in PreK-Grade 12 classrooms.*
5. *Offer professional learning for educators, diagnosticians, etc., on how to incorporate authentic bilingual assessment in multilingual settings for all learners.*

Ali Fuad Selvi, Associate Professor of TESOL and Applied Linguistics, University of Alabama, also reminds us of the importance of

> *the deliberate and equitable affirmation, representation, and integration of students' multilingual repertoires in educational settings in terms of policy, pedagogy, and teacher preparation. In educational contexts with a heightened sense of multilingual justice, languages are respected as integral to learners' identities and development. Thus, the ultimate goal of education in such contexts is additive multilingualism/plurilingualism.*

Pause for a Moment

Are dual language education programs currently available for multilingual learners in your district?
Who gets to participate?
What systemic supports are in place to make access to dual language programming equitable?

FAMILY AND COMMUNITY ENGAGEMENT
CULTIVATE MULTILINGUAL JUSTICE IN EVERY WAY IN EVERY PLACE
STUDENT-TO-STUDENT TEACHER-TO-STUDENT AND TEACHER-TO-TEACHER COLLABORATION

Cultivating Collaborative Pathways to Multilingual Equity and Justice

Multilingualism does not grow and blossom in a vacuum. Meaningful, authentic interactions on every possible level of education are necessary for it to develop. Let's start by examining the role student-to-student, teacher-to-student, and teacher-to-teacher collaboration plays in ensuring multilingual justice.

I grew up and became a teacher in a highly collectivistic culture in Eastern Europe. At times, I joke that sharing and collaboration are my middle name it is so much a part of who I am as a person, an educator, and an advocate for social justice and equity for multilingual learners. When I started my career as a middle school English as a Foreign Language (EFL) teacher in Debrecen, Hungary, I had almost as much time to plan and collaborate with colleagues built into my schedule as teaching students the intricacies of the English language. Collaboration followed me to the New York City Public Schools, where I was among the first English as a Second Language (ESL) teachers to follow the example of the special education inclusion model and coteach. I have offered professional learning sessions, conference presentations, webinars, podcasts and other resources on the topic of teacher collaboration, contributed to policy documents published by NYSED and WIDA and have numerous articles and books published. Here, I challenge myself to offer you the most essential recommendations I have for making collaboration a multi-layered, equity-oriented practice that contributes to cultivating equity.

Tapestry of Voices

Tim Boals, WIDA Founder and Senior Principal Investigator at University of Wisconsin, also underscores the importance of collaboration:

We have to get science, math, and social studies teachers on board. It's so much more than just learning English; it's being able to navigate the whole school. They need to understand the language acquisition process at some level, and they need to understand how culture comes into play so that they can make their content classes more accessible and more supported. We really want to get to the point where all of our multilingual learners are succeeding. It takes the whole village. It takes everybody in the school. That's why collaboration is so important! We must have ESL/ELD and bilingual teachers collaborating with the content area teachers, and everybody understanding what the needs are. That's the way you create schools where kids are having successful experiences.

Student-to-Student Collaboration

In the sociocultural tradition, languages only grow and develop when they are used purposefully for meaning making and developing higher order thinking (Vygotsky, 1978). While we want to nurture independence and self-directed learning, students are preparing for a networked, collaborative society. While we want to ensure students act with agency and autonomy, they also need to learn to interact, communicate, solve problems, and achieve shared goals with others.

Walking through so many school buildings and classrooms as I have done in the past two decades, I often pause and read inspirational quotes, messages, posters, and other reminders posted on classroom and hallway walls revealing what is being valued by the community. Let me now take you to a magical space with me.

In this linguistic-minded world, all the quotes in the box below are about the importance of talk. Which one talks about you? Which one talks to you? Which one could be on a poster?

The Importance of Talk

> Whoever teaches learns in the act of teaching, and whoever learns teaches in the act of learning.
>
> (Paulo Freire, 1998, p. 31)

> Reading and writing float on a sea of talk.
>
> (James Britton, 1983, p. 11)

> Whoever explains, learns.
>
> (David Sousa, 2022, p. 86)

> It's all about the talk.
>
> (Nancy Frey, Douglas Fisher, & John Nelson, 2013, p. 8)

> Be brave enough to start a conversation that matters.
>
> (Margaret Wheatley, 2009, p. 163)

> More than we realize, we are the products of thousands of conversations.
>
> (Jeff Zwiers & Marie Crawford, 2024, p. 1)

However, a really important question is, who is doing the talking? Whose perspectives, wisdoms and languages are heard? At the core of all learning is student voice, active participation, and critical engagement—engagement with the content, with academic language and literacy practices, and with students' and their peers' authentic selves. Amanda Kibler et al. (2021) suggest that "critical and dialogic educational practices provide a space for students to learn through multiple voices and perspectives" (p. xiii). Students need to interact through all modalities, all modes of communication, and all the languages of their choice. They need to interact with their English-speaking peers and same-language partners, interact with their teachers and other adults in the classroom and school community and beyond. Multilingual learners should not be silent or silenced.

When students actively participate in academic conversations, they use their full linguistic repertoires, demonstrate their understanding, share new learning, or present their ideas through multilingual and multimodal forms of expression. See some examples how to do that across the four core content areas and beyond but consider many more ways to cultivate multilingualism.

- In language arts, students select and discuss non-fiction and fiction pieces of literature that are relevant to their lives and share their own lived experiences; students and their teachers embrace multiliteracies as they jointly explore multimedia resources, videoclips, and films in addition to print-based materials.
- In social studies, students pose their own questions, establish shared lines of inquiry, participate in debates and critical conversations around issues students sincerely care about.
- In math, students engage in talk about math problems, explain their thinking, make connections between abstract concepts and real-life scenarios where math matters (and, yes, also why they will never need to use those concepts in real life).
- In science, students engage in task-based discussions that build on hands-on explorations and multiple representations such as diagrams, outlines, sketches, and video-recorded responses as well as in inquiry that provides additional opportunities for disciplinary conversations about cross-cutting concepts.
- In visual arts, students describe both their plans for their work, the processes they engaged in, and share their final creations.
- In music, students share their personal, familial, cultural, and linguistic experiences with music and songs related to the lesson.

Multilingual learners must have ample opportunities to negotiate meaning through authentic, critical conversations in multiple languages. Actively fighting any attempts of tracking or segregating multilingual learners within a district, school, or even inside a classroom are powerful ways you can cultivate multilingual justice.

Notable Research

Peggy Estrada, Haiwen Wang, and Timea Farkas (2020) studied classroom-level student segregation and student achievement over three years in an elementary school context and reported the following:

After accounting for student-, classroom-, and school-level covariates, we found that ELs [English learners] in more segregated classrooms exhibited lower performance, on average, on state tests of English language arts, mathematics, and English proficiency, and little evidence that classroom number of EL English proficiency levels was related to achievement. School staff consistently detailed the instructional, academic, and socio-emotional opportunities to learn afforded by the diversity/heterogeneity of integrated classrooms.

(Estrada et al., 2020, p. 1792)

Students' multilingualism will only be cultivated if all their languages are actively and authentically being used. See Table 5.3 for a summary chart of different types of student interactions, the main purposes of each, possible group structures, and how multilingual equity may better connect to all types of grouping configurations.

Tapestry of Voices

Jeff Zwiers, author and former senior researcher at the Stanford Graduate School of Education, emphasizes the need for rich communication and idea building in the classroom:

What's missing in my mind, both in classrooms and in assessments, is one aspect of communication—are we asking kids to share their brilliance? What I've been focused on a lot lately is to give them opportunities to share their ideas and to keep building them, using both school learning and their own personal backgrounds, experiences, and ways of communicating. I want them to say the second sentence. It doesn't have to be complete, I just want them to get started on that second sentence.

Table 5.3 Types of interactions, purposes, group structures, and multilingual equity.

	Peer-to-peer	**Small group**	**Whole class**
What does each interaction look like?	Two students work together to accomplish a task, complete an activity, or work through a problem	Three to five students collaborate to complete a task or activity	The teacher engages with all students simultaneously, requiring participation from the entire class
What are the main purposes of each?	To engage in peer teaching and learning To participate in shorter or more sustained collaborative tasks To build confidence while interacting with one partner	To encourage diverse perspectives To develop collaboration skills To experience a safe, supportive learning environment To learn from others while sharing own strengths	To build class community To share diverse ideas To explore divergent thinking patterns To practice public speaking
What are some possible group structures?	Random pairing Ability-based pairing Mixed proficiency pairing	Mixed-ability/ proficiency grouping Interest-based groups Task-specific groups	Flexible seating arrangements Panel discussion Debate team
How can we focus multilingual equity across all group configurations?	• Integrating multilingual resources including print and digital materials and scaffolds • Leveraging students' multiple languages while they engage with same language and mixed language peers • Inviting interactive presentations with collaborative discussions, problem-solving and writing tasks • Offering jigsaw activities where students' cultural and linguistic expertise are centered		

Source: adapted from Dove et al. (2026, p. 291)

Teacher-to-Student Collaboration

Long gone are the days when the primary mode of teaching is by direct instruction and the role of teachers is defined as taking control over a class. Instead, we "learn *from, about,* and *with* our students by redefining and celebrating teaching and learning as a joint, collaborative process in which students are teachers and teachers are learners" (Honigsfeld et al., 2022, p. 58).

Multilingual learners thrive in an environment that is built on high levels of relational trust with caring adults. Redefining the power dynamic in classrooms with multilingual learners shifts the roles and positions students and teachers tend to take: Students are viewed as knowers and teachers embrace their role as learners. When teachers and students forge a partnership with the shared goal of fair and just learning for all, they accomplish all the following and much more:

- Building bridges that foster communication and mutual understanding.
- Discussing and establishing a shared purpose of learning that reflects inclusive values of peers, teachers, and parents.
- Creating routines and structures that honor multilingual participation and engagement.
- Advocating on behalf of multilingual learners.

Teachers and students may collaborate in and outside the classroom in numerous ways. One emerging approach in educational research is called Youth Participatory Action Research or YPAR. It is a kind of innovative inquiry project that centers young people in investigating an issue that personally impacts them or their communities. Adults such as teachers or researchers provide mentorship and guidance, but the participating youth determine all the key elements of their research project (see https://yparhub.berkeley.edu for more information).

Notable Research

Deborah Palmer, Laura Meinzen, Maya Milán, and Michelle Renée Valladares (2025) report on how engaging multilingual learners in action research accomplishes multiple interrelated goals, such as jointly exploring language policies and how they impact students, supporting their bilingual and biliteracy development, enhancing their communication and research skills, as well as inspiring both students and their educator partners to become advocates:

> *Building solidarity and identity negotiation within the messiness of our co-constructed bilingual space, plus having an authentic pathway to take action, enabled our students to further develop their own critical consciousness and their understandings of themselves as language policy actors, not to mention their data collection, analysis, and synthesis skills—and their biliteracy! Through multilingual YPAR, students engaged in the process of their own becoming, meaning making, and critical consciousness development.*
>
> (Palmer et al., 2025, pp. 9–10)

Tapestry of Voices

Diane Staehr Fenner, author and president of SupportEd, highlights the importance of relationship building and developing a sense of belonging for multilingual learners through the following actions:

- ★ *Intentionally creating a space where MLs feel safe and welcome, which includes teachers forming relationships with MLs and encouraging student-student relationships.*
- ★ *Ensuring MLs are integrated with non-MLs throughout the school day so that they are not segregated from the general population and have opportunities to hear and learn English from peers.*

Teacher-to-Teacher Collaboration

Teacher collaboration holds a special promise for multilingual learners and for multilingual equity for a range of reasons. Collaboration among educators is expected to ensure:

- ◆ Reduction in fragmented, disjointed learning experiences for multilingual learners.
- ◆ Less student isolation and more meaningful integration into the classroom and school community.
- ◆ Curriculum continuity across classrooms and grade levels with special attention to multilingual, multicultural experiences.
- ◆ Instructional consistency that values multilingualism, nurtures translanguaging pedagogies, and integrates content, language, and social-emotional development.

Cultivating purposeful teacher collaboration around multilingual justice begins with developing a range of competencies: understanding of the expectations for teamwork, the use of data-informed instruction, fidelity to congruent and inclusive learning experiences for all students, and the commitment to work to achieve equity.

There is a growing understanding that collective teacher efficacy and collaborative expertise are critical for student success. The most compelling evidence in support of teacher collaboration has emerged from the work of John Hattie (2018), who recognized the power of collective efficacy and the importance of collaborative expertise. As a result, meaningful and sustained teacher collaboration—sharing successful instructional strategies, examining student data, reflecting on effective teaching practices, and so on—must be prioritized. When teachers collaborate and form high-functioning teams, their collective efficacy—their belief in their collaborative effectiveness—is increased (Donohoo & Katz, 2019). See Figure 5.1 to recognize what collaborating educators may share with each other.

Family and Community Engagement through Collaboration

My next call to action is to cultivate a lasting partnership with families and communities. When we see, hear and recognize our multilingual learner's immediate and extended families as a resource, we reach out to them, we partner with them and we invite them to help make important decisions about their children's academic, linguistic, and social-emotional growth. On the other hand, when families see the school as a place to trust, critical community relationships are forged in which multilingualism is accepted, valued, and fully embraced.

Joyce Epstein and colleagues (2019) identified two powerful phenomena they refer to as:

1. Family-like schools: educators and all school personnel know and value children for who they are just like their own families, parents, caregivers, and relatives would.
2. School-like families—caregivers and other family members embrace their role and responsibility in supporting children's education to the best of their ability and work in collaboration with educators and all other service providers within the school system.

In family-like schools, we celebrate each child's gift, talent, spirit just as their caring families do, including sharing the rich cultural and linguistic heritages and living practices. Similarly, in school-like families, parents are engaged in authentic, extended learning opportunities along with their children,

What Do Educators Who Collaborate Share With Each Other?

1. Pedagogical Knowledge
    a. Child and adolescent development and the learning process
    b. Teaching methods based on contemporary theory and current research
    c. Unit and lesson planning and assessment practices
    d. Student engagement and classroom management skills
    e. ______________________________
2. Content Expertise
    a. Comprehensive knowledge of the subject matter
    b. In-depth familiarity with the core curriculum
    c. National and state content and ELD standards
    d. Strategies aligned to grade-appropriate content learning
    e. ______________________________
3. Language Acquisition and Literacy Development Processes
    a. Stages of language acquisition
    b. Multimodal and multilingual approaches to language and literacy instruction
    c. Culturally and linguistically responsive and sustaining literacy learning
    d. High expectations with multidimensional scaffolding
    e. ______________________________
4. Cross-Cultural Understanding
    a. Awareness of cultural norms and respect for cultural differences
    b. Empathy and perspective-taking
    c. Combating stereotypes, bias, and prejudice
    d. Fostering trust and relationships with students and their families
    e. ______________________________
5. Interpersonal Skills
    a. Communication skills (You can talk to me . . .)
    b. Relationship building (You can count on me . . .)
    c. Encouragement (I have an idea . . .)
    d. Inspiration (I can help . . .)
    e. ______________________________

Figure 5.1 What do educators who collaborate share with each other?

such as place-based project-based learning, family oral histories, and so on. Building these dynamic two-way relationships are expected to lead to increased self-confidence for students, stronger connections to school-life, more engaged families, and multiple sources of support for the multilingual learner.

Key initial strategies to cultivate collaborative partnerships with families include:

- Seeking input from parents when designing culturally and linguistically responsive and sustaining curriculum and instruction for their children.
- Encouraging parents to share how their children learn best.
- Embracing the rich linguistic, literacy, and cultural experiences and assets.
- Ensuring that the community becomes a core source of information and support.
- Recruiting community liaisons with strong community connections, competent in the language and culture of the people in the community, people the community trusts.

When multilingual families feel more confident in the school community, we can further cultivate some family engagement practices, such as:

- Provide free workshops (in multiple languages) for parents to learn about the services offered both within and outside the school.
- Offer free adult education classes to support language learning.
- Provide parents with multilingual resources to support them in advocating for their children's education, mental health, and social emotional wellbeing.
- Create multilingual libraries in the buildings to give greater access to literacy resources.

The importance of actively engaging multilingual families in their children's education cannot be stressed enough. It starts by providing accessible communication, interpretation, and translation services, and ensuring participation in decision-making processes. Cultivating multilingual justice, however, must go beyond providing access; it ensures that families are fully informed, empowered, and seen as partners who share in equitable decision-making.

Pause for a Moment

Which collaborative partnership opportunities are most predominant in your context (student-to-student, teacher-to-student, teacher-to-teacher, family, and community collaborations)?

Give an example for each from your school or district. Which type of collaborations would need to be cultivated further and why?

Spotlight on Multilingual Justice

Cornelius Godfrey (Diversity & Equity consultant), Christy Osborne (English Language Development (ELD) consultant), Christina Kozlowski (ELD consultant), and Kelsey Witt (Newcomer English Learner consultant) serve as consultants at the county intermediate school district (ISD) in Southeast Michigan with 28 school districts and 26 Public School Academies ranging from less than 1000 up to almost 15,000 students enrolled. The team share their story of "A Radical Dream and Resilience through Challenge":

> Our families speak over 100 languages, and our schools are situated in some of the most affluent communities in the United States while others serve students with 100% Title I eligibility. Our desire was to center the often-silenced voice of multilingual learners (ML) in the systems that serve them. Our hearts were all radically dreaming (Dugan, 2022) a similar vision of multilingual and other marginalized students working alongside educators to co-design educational systems with student agency and equity as starting points. Since we do not directly work with students, our primary role is to build educator capacity. Previously collected county data showed a need for sustained and integrated work around diversity, equity and inclusion (DEI) and multilingual justice; we hoped a partnership would serve as a model. This resulted in aligned educator and student-facing initiatives (see Figure 5.2): two large-scale

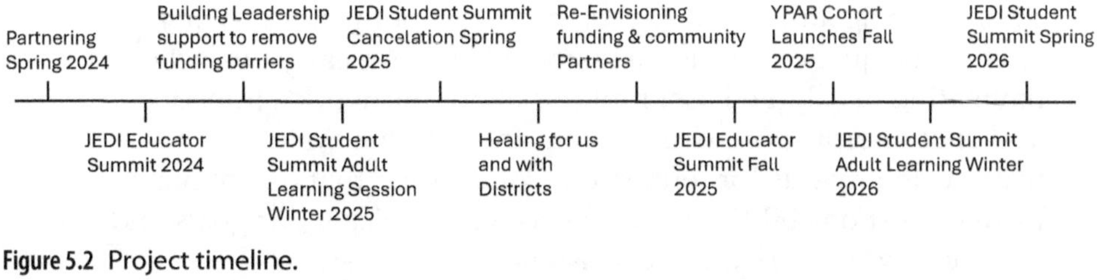

Figure 5.2 Project timeline.

conferences, the Justice, Equity, Diversity and Inclusion (JEDI) Educator and Student Summits, professional learning, and a cohort of educators engaging in co-creating student projects through the Youth Participatory Action Research framework (YPAR) (https://yparhub.berkeley.edu).

Early in our teamwork, we spent a significant amount of our time learning, exploring ideas and research, calibrating our thinking, and honing our purpose. We felt clarity around seeking the margins of school communities (Safir & Dugan, 2021), especially those with linguistic, racial, and ethnic diversity. Our collaboration allowed us to name how our intentional partnership between ML and DEI work could impact the educational environments for all our diverse students.

As the larger sociopolitical context shifted to position the immigrant community further at the margins, our team's purpose was galvanized. We found solidarity and hope, which gave us the resilience we needed as challenges arose. In response, we developed our non-negotiables:

- ★ Intentional adult learning
- ★ Opportunities to co-design meaningful change with students
- ★ Integration of ML and DEI communities
- ★ Elimination of financial barriers to participation
- ★ Foundation in research-based practices (YPAR)

We started by front loading our adult collaborators (and ourselves) with learning opportunities that would challenge the adult dispositions that could sabotage authentic youth agency. Additionally, we created structures that specifically invited ML educators and students into DEI work and removed any financial burdens for district attendees.

The JEDI student summit required us to pave a path that didn't previously exist, so our first task was not planning logistics, but establishing multiple levels of partnership. Obstacles were disappointing, but not unexpected, at least not when viewing educational justice through a historical lens. An early obstacle was navigating misaligned assumptions about our work's intended audience and purpose with leaders and internal systems. This became an impetus for refinement. We learned that one of our primary responsibilities would be to communicate our goals and intentions with clarity and consistency.

J.E.D.I. Educator Summit

November 6, 2025: in person
Audience: All are welcome
The event centers on fostering a deeper understanding of Justice, Equity, Diversity, and Inclusion within K-12 education and beyond.
Registration Link. Flyer Link.

Oakland County YPAR Cohort-Apply now!

Accepting applications now through November 12th (MISTEM partnership).
Audience: Educators who support grades 2-12, J.E.D.I. Student Summit adult sponsors, 3P Leaders, and District/School staff focused on DEI initiatives
Advanced opportunity to dig deeper through YPAR ongoing coursework with Dr. Barnett's online course through EMU. Description of course; Cohort application

J.E.D.I. Student Summit

February 10, 2026 Adult learning prior to Summit
April 30, 2026: in person district teams, Flyer Link
District teams of adult sponsors and student leaders gather to learn and grow in YPAR and advocacy in their contexts. Participation details coming soon.

J.E.D.I. Academy Cohorts & Community of Practice

Join the J.E.D.I. Academy listserv for ongoing information throughout the 2025-26 school year

Figure 5.3 Timeline of events in the second year of the project.

By holding firm in our non-negotiables and asking hard questions of ourselves and our system, we could move beyond the status quo. This new territory resulted in a communication plan with all levels of district and county leaders (see Figure 5.3). Newfound support led to an event in April 2025 that was fully funded; all district educators and students would attend for free which was the largest barrier to equitable access across our county. Increased communication with district superintendents was key to building district partnerships as we moved into our second annual summits.

Even with supportive leadership, challenges persisted: state and federal funding sources, system structures, and the growing sociopolitical tensions impacting educational institutions. Our organization faced the complex task of making decisions which impact communities with diverse demographics, priorities, and pressures. Just weeks prior to the first JEDI student summit, national pressures threatening the removal of federal funding from schools engaging in DEI initiatives increased. Our leadership, to prevent possible loss of federal funds to schools, made the difficult decision to cancel the event.

Afterwards, we spent necessary time healing as a team and restoring relational trust with districts. We embarked on reenvisioning and expanding our work by connecting with our community partners: Discover without Barriers Consulting (https://discoverwithoutbarriers.org) and our Michigan STEM (MiSTEM) regional director (MiSTEM Network, n.d.). This shift allowed for educators, in various roles and districts, to join the first county-wide YPAR educator cohort. Together we committed to learn, grow our practices, and initiate student-led projects centered on making meaningful change in learning communities.

By sharing our story, we hope to illuminate some of our learning as we applied the intersection of DEI, student agency, and multilingual justice in our context (see Figure 5.4). We are continuing our journey to grow in pursuit of student agency in designing equitable learning environments.

Insights and actions that strategically moved our work forward:

- Engaging in dialogue, shared learning, and radical dreaming to maintain our unity as a team and clarify our non-negotiables
- Co-creating and sustaining an ongoing journey towards equitable, bias-free learning environments with our districts
- Utilizing data to examine existing systems and structures to prioritize the work
- Aligning goals across team partnerships, community partners, and districts
- Remaining resilient through challenges without giving up hope or complying to pressures prematurely
- Maintaining a flexible mindset to move forward in both the short- and long-term visions through the current challenges
- Continually inviting leaders and colleagues into the work; expanding understanding and partnerships to remove silos

Figure 5.4 Lessons learned.

Moving Beyond Cultivating Multilingual Justice

Cultivating multilingual justice is a long-term commitment with many intertwined components. Just like tending to a plant to grow, equity is not a single initiative or a short-term project, it requires time and concerted collaborative effort. The next chapter will address how to sustain multilingual equity by creating and sustaining equitable classrooms, schools, and districts where multilingualism is the norm.

End-of-Chapter Reflections

As you finish exploring the fourth ability of equity literacy, reflect on the following:

- What specific policies and plans are already in place in your Lau Plan that center multilingual learners and fully honor multilingualism?
- What program models are available for multilingual learners and how can multilingualism be further recognized and integrated in them?
- What refinements or additions to existing program models should be made?
- How can collaboration on all levels permeate the school culture to advance multilingual justice?

6

How to Sustain Multilingual Equity and Justice

Defining and Living a Linguistically Just Mission and Vision

Having grown up and lived in Hungary for the first half of my life, I often looked to Eastern European thought leaders and authors who might be less commonly known in the United States, such as Václav Havel, Milan Kundera, Kertész Imre, Heller Ágnes and others. One formidable message that has stayed with me over the years is attributed to Václav Havel. I appreciate the way he captures the essence of how foresights, dreams or visions are not impactful without action. The following translation of his ideas is not only a powerful play on words but a continued inspiration for me:

> Vision is not enough, it must be combined with venture. It is not enough to stare up the steps, we must step up the stairs.

Tapestry of Voices

Julie Esparza Brown, Professor at Portland State University, passionately underscores the need for taking sustained steps to ensure that multilingual justice becomes a reality.

Justice must be thought of as an action. Justice is the action of ensuring that resources, opportunities, and fair treatment are equitably available to everyone. To me, multilingual justice means giving opportunities

DOI: 10.4324/9781003644071-6

so that all individuals can be multilingual by providing a continuum of supports based on the linguistic assets each person brings. The opposite of this is what is common across the country—asking people, particularly children, to leave their home language at the school door and only learn the "national" language. This robs students of their full potential.

To be fully inclusive of multilingual learners in all aspects of school life will require intentional, sustained work. Granted, pushbacks and challenges are likely to arise along the way, so clarity of priorities that include multilingualism and deliberate daily actions (Safir & Dugan, 2021) are needed to advance multilingual justice. Mission and vision statements are a powerful place to establish those priorities, to review and revise them from time to time, and to align everything that happens in a school or district to them. Since the two are frequently mentioned together and the line between visions and missions might even be blurry at times, I call on Alan Blankstein's powerful explanation to help clarify how the two differ:

> *Whereas the mission statement reminds us why we exist, a vision paints a picture of what we can become. … a school's vision should guide the collective direction of its stakeholders. It should provide a compelling sense of where the school is headed and, in broad terms, what must be accomplished in the future to fulfill the school's purpose. Every decision made, every program implemented, every policy instituted, and all goals should align with this vision.*
>
> (Blankstein, 2013, p. 94)

If the mission is the "why" and the vision is the "how" a school or district operates, it is critical to ensure that multilingual learners are included in both. Are they there, though?

Pause for a Moment

Is multilingualism recognized as a core value in your context?
Is linguistic diversity acknowledged and appreciated?
Are any of the mission and vision statements, core value statements or multi-year strategic plans published on your district's website inclusive of multilingual learners?

If you think that we are not there yet, I must agree! We have a lot more important work to do to ensure that in addition to developing all the equity literacy abilities presented in the previous chapters—*recognizing, responding to, redressing* and *cultivating* multilingual equity and justice—we can sustain equity and justice for multilingual learners. I was also wondering if any large-scale studies have been conducted to help answer the questions I raised above in a more scientific and systemic way.

Sponsored by the Pew Research Center, Meltem Odabaş and Carolina Aragão (2022) investigated the educational priorities and commitments expressed in 1500 randomly selected mission and vision statements representative of varied geographic and political regions such as urban, suburban and rural districts in Republican and Democratic leaning areas. Of the numerous predictable patterns that emerged, only about 34% of school districts identify their efforts regarding diversity, equity and inclusion, while the most common features of these statements focus generically on future readiness, safe and healthy learning environments, parent and community involvement, and academic skills. They cautioned that since 2022, contents of mission statements might have changed and some of the results might no longer hold up. What struck me the most was a lack of any specific mention of linguistic diversity and multilingualism in the Center's actual report. The absence of multilingual learners in the research study is just as concerning as the lack of their inclusion in district level mission and vision statements.

I had to do my own search, albeit not as comprehensive a study as the Pew Center's one. I examined dozens of school district mission statements from around the United States that were accessible publicly on their websites. I was looking for evidence of acknowledging linguistic diversity and noting the importance of multilingualism—I wonder if you are ready to take a guess about what I found … They are rarely if ever included. Occasionally, there are references to students' or families' multinational origins or the importance of celebrating cultural diversity. Other times, there is a commitment to fostering global citizenship and cross-cultural understanding. Yet in many others, there is no mention of multilingualism and no connection made to the rich linguistic heritage of the community. So, it was most affirming to see this short excerpt in a mission statement published by a large urban school district in which both inequities connected to linguistic barriers and the need for school and community collaboration are highlighted:

> *Our city is enriched and strengthened by its diverse cultural heritage and multinational population. Within our classrooms and neighborhoods, and on our stages and athletic fields, we want learning to be relevant and connected to developing our students into value-centered citizens who are able*

to navigate a complex and inequitable world. We aim to address these inequities—including racism, socio-economic status and language barriers—to create an environment in which every child can and will succeed. We want our students to feel safe taking academic risks while mindfully respecting diversity of opinions. To do so, we must foster supportive and collaborative partnerships between families, the community, and the school district so that every child reaches a high level of achievement. The foundation of our work is collaboration, mutual respect, and high expectations, where all educators are reflective of their practice and feel supported as they continually adjust instruction to improve student performance.

Since district-level searches yielded little affirmation of multilingualism, I looked to school-based mission and vision statements. When an entire school is designed to provide dual language or bilingual education, the school-specific mission statements powerfully reflect such a commitment. There are numerous examples of such schools, see one instance of how an academy in the southwest centers multilingualism throughout their statement:

[ ] Academy is a K-8 school that provides an opportunity for all students to achieve high levels of bilingual proficiency and to develop multicultural competency through a rigorous English and Spanish dual language immersion instruction program. Our school philosophy is based on the belief that, one who knows two languages can contribute in two worlds." Within this philosophical framework, [______] values and respects both languages and all cultures equally, instills a sense of community service in students, develops future leaders, and involves parents as part of the school learning community.

Similarly, an international school in an urban area in southern US proudly claims in their mission statement that they fully embrace multilingualism and establish cross-cultural competence as goals for their school community:

Our mission as a community is to inspire students to become multilingual global citizens who pursue a lifelong journey of discovery and action where the quest for deep academic knowledge and an appreciation of world cultures contribute to the advancement of humanity.

After reviewing dozens of statements, I have noted a powerful trend through this informal investigation. Most frequently, schools and districts might not address multilingual learners or language-based equity directly, multilingual departments within a school district must feel compelled to craft their own mission and vision statements as a way to affirm their belief in, and commitment to, nurturing and sustaining multilingualism. There was no shortage of departmental statements across all geographic regions promoting bilingualism, emphasizing inclusivity, or reassuring members of the community that languages are seen as assets and families are partners. See how a department in a small suburban district outlines their equity-oriented core values in addition to the mission and vision statements:

Mission

We will welcome and educate all by …

- *Respecting culturally and linguistically diverse students by leveraging their native language and background to create a strengths-based instructional model.*
- *Providing a high quality, comprehensive, and equitable education for all.*
- *Using research-based instruction, collaborative spaces, and reflective practices.*
- *Developing academic language across the four language domains to support student success in school and beyond.*
- *Engaging families and the community as partners in our students' education.*

Vision

- *The educators and students of the [____] Department are a diverse community of empowered learners who are able to transform the world around us.*

Core Values

- *Honoring linguistic and cultural assets*
- *Equity*
- *Community and collaboration*
- *Perseverance*
- *Respect*

Finally, let's look at one more paired vision and mission statement from a large near-urban district's multilingual department located in the northwestern part of the United States. The call to embrace an anti-racist, social justice stance on behalf of multilingual learners, families, educators, and community members gives me hope and affirms the importance of equity work focused on multilingualism:

Multilingual Department Vision Statement:

- *To affirm and inspire each and every student to learn and thrive as creators of their future world while celebrating their cultural, racial, and linguistic identities.*

Multilingual Department Mission Statement:

- *As the multilingual learners' department, we commit to being anti-racist by promoting educational, linguistic, and racial equity for our students, families, educators, and community members. We engage in high-quality culturally relevant and rigorous educational practices that uphold respect, non-discrimination, and fairness. As social justice advocates, we affirm student identity, promote multilingualism through an additive mindset, and structure our work for integration of all voices.*

To guide your work on reviewing and revising mission, vision, and core values statements, I recommend that you and your team look to the community: first and foremost, to the multilingual community in your own district as well as the professional community supporting multilingualism. Professional organizations whose primary focus is on multilingualism will have powerful mission statements, such as TESOL, WIDA, AAAL, ACTFL. However, numerous other professional organizations in education and related fields have also crafted position statements specially addressing linguistic diversity and multilingual learners, such as NCTE, NCTM, NAYEC, ASHA, ILA, CEC, just to name a few. Check the organizations that you are most involved in and look for commitment to multilingual equity. If there is current evidence of such statements, find out how you can get actively involved to advance the cause; if there is not, advocate to ensure that there will be one.

Pause for a Moment

These mission and vision statements underscore the pronounced need for them to be inclusive of multilingual learners. What message is sent to the larger community about the mission statements of the districts, schools and multilingual departments you have reviewed?

What spoke to you in each statement and why?
What do the mission and vision statements in your district, school, and multilingual department say about multilingualism and multilingual learners?
What else could or should be stated, cultivated, and enacted and why?

Tapestry of Voices

David Rogers, language educator and advocate, offers three overarching approaches to sustaining equity efforts, one of which is also closely aligned to mission and vision statements, namely to articulate and enact organizational values:

Approach 1: When changes are proposed (i.e. in policy or practice) that can lead to inequity, be prepared to point out what the outcome (intentional or unintentional) could be for increasing inequity.
Approach 2: Develop a plan, guide, etc. with the community that clearly presents values and intent (mission) of the organization that can help all members avoid unintentionally weakening the commitment to equity.
Approach 3: Have an identified group of people (i.e. equity councils) who are ready, willing and able to analyze any pending decision to ensure that it won't lead to greater inequity and/or follows the plan from Approach two.

Not only

Not only on crisp paper, but in actions as well!
Not only on glaring computer screens, but in actions as well!
Not only in overstuffed folders, but in actions as well!
Not only in brimming binders, but in actions as well!
Not only on shiny posters, but in actions as well!

Sustained Equity Work for Multilingual Justice

In Chapter 3, I explored how actions along with words respond to multilingual inequities and injustices. Those immediate and shorter-term actions are necessary to confront inequities, to offer quick interventions, to improve relationships, but they might be lacking in lasting impact. Here my focus is on actions that may also be viewed as sustained efforts, relentless undertakings, courageous endeavors, daring attainments, and successful accomplishments! To reach such a level of equity literacy where the greatest challenge is to sustain multilingual justice is no small feat!

Tapestry of Voices

Kevin Wong, Associate Professor and Chair of MA in TESOL program, Pepperdine University, Los Angeles, California, also recognizes the complexity of equity work:

- ★ *Build coalitions and allyship by forming diverse equity teams.*
- ★ *Embed equity into policies, job expectations, and resource allocation.*
- ★ *Provide continuous professional learning that prepares educators to stay committed to equity work.*
- ★ *Center the perspectives of marginalized students and families.*

Chris Montecillo Leider, Assistant Professor, School of Education, University of Massachusetts, Lowell, MA, also calls for action to achieve multilingual justice by:

- ★ *Abolishing dominant or official language only policies (and long-standing practices masquerading as policies).*
- ★ *Creating sustainable and funded pathways to becoming teachers for multilingual racialized populations.*

> ★ *Establishing bilingual education (two-way and one-way DLBE) programs.*
> ★ *Providing students with opportunities to learn content in a language beyond the dominant or official language even in more traditional dominant/official language models.*
> ★ *Offering translation services and live interpretation.*

Some of the equity efforts I am ready to share next are practiced daily or frequently; others might only be emerging practices, yet others are examples of how to dream big and bold. I continue to center multilingual learners so I will start with them. What can all students do to sustain equity and justice for multilingualism? Next, I explore what educators and non-instructional staff members can do. I will move on to how members of administrative and instructional leadership teams contribute to sustaining multilingual justice and equity at local, regional and state levels. Recognizing their roles and responsibilities with a strong sense of urgency, what policy makers and school boards can do will also be addressed. And to come to full circle, I will return to the multilingual community, such as caregivers' and family members' engagement in advocacy and action for equity and justice (see Figure 6.1).

What Multilingual Learners Can Do Sustain Multilingual Justice and Equity

Multilingual learners must hold on to their rich cultural and linguistic heritages and fully embrace their intersectional identities. Not to be ashamed, not to hide, not to give up who they are! As they do so, they successfully build their personal and academic agency, take ownership of their learning, and take charge of their multilingual future. In many cases, it might be easier said than done! Multilingual youths thrive when family and community support helps them maintain their languages and expand their linguistic assets. They also need educators who believe in them and in the power of their multilingualism.

When multilingual learners can leverage their linguistic and cultural funds of knowledge and funds of identities (reflective of their personal, familial, and cultural lived experiences), they recognize that they matter. It matters what they say and how they say it. Not only do they matter, what students do, and how they share their varied ways of knowing and learning are valued.

Multilingual learners are well positioned to share their richness of language and culture by …

- ◆ Connecting their lived experiences to curriculum and instruction.
- ◆ Sharing their linguistic expertise.
- ◆ Representing multilingual multicultural community resources.

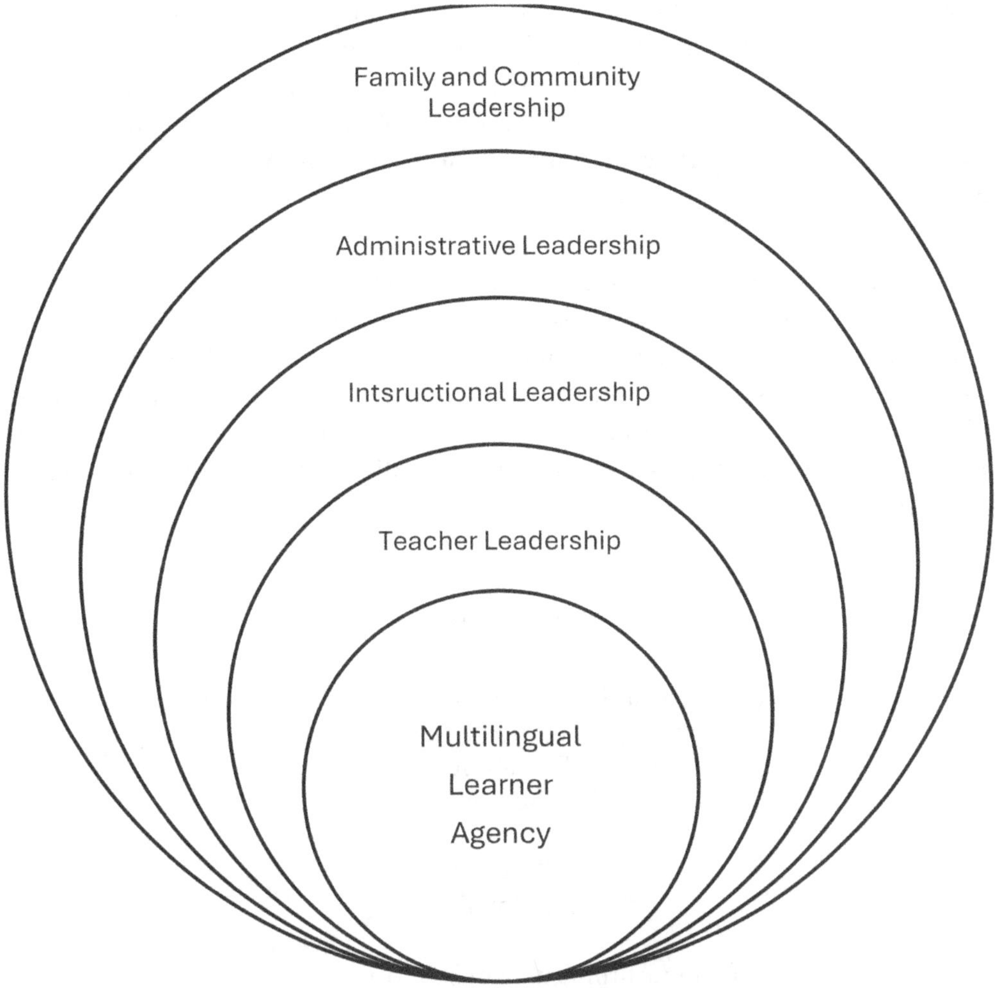

Figure 6.1 Leadership layers to sustain multilingual justice and equity.

- Mentoring other multilingual learners.
- Assuming student leadership roles to be able to advocate for multilingual equity.
- ____
- ____

(I invite you to continue the list by inviting student and teacher input.)

In addition, with support and encouragement, they are likely to achieve the Seal of Biliteracy. Since its inception in California in 2008, all 50 states have joined the movement and now offer the Seal of Biliteracy, all students in all schools can vie for this honor to be added to their high school diploma. Every year, when I am asked to be an examiner for a student or two in New

York State I enthusiastically say yes. Not only because I know how hard it is for districts to find qualified professionals to offer this exam in less commonly spoken languages, but I also do it for the joy of engaging young people in honoring students' and their families' efforts to maintain their home language and develop literacy without formal education offered within the public school system.

What All Students Can Do to Sustain Multilingual Justice and Equity

All students—multilingual learners and others who might be, aspiring to be, will be multilingual (or might remain monolingual for now)—play a role in creating an inclusive, welcoming environment where all languages are valued. Students support each other in their private and public use of the language of their preference, rather than discouraging or disparaging multilingualism.

Dis-ing Multilingualism

Champion multilingualism as a gift, an asset, so it
never gets treated as a source of
DIS-ability
DIS-advantage
DIS-order
DIS-unity
DIS-loyalty

Affirm multilingualism so it does not get
DIS-regarded
DIS-owned
DIS-respected
DIS-couraged

Center multilingualism,
So, it does not disappear
So, it is never disapproved, discounted, disputed,
disguised, dismantled.

Uplift multilingualism,
So, it is discussed, disambiguated, discerned, displayed,
discovered, distinguished.

All students including monolingual learners can advance multilingual equity by …

- Challenging their own and others' English-only mindset in day-to-day instructional and assessment practices.
- Rejecting a deficit-oriented view of others who are learning English or do not speak the dominant language of the school or community.
- Actively pursuing language studies and aiming for bilingualism or multilingualism in their own educational endeavors.
- Researching and embracing their own cultural and linguistic histories and heritages.
- Respecting an increasingly diverse linguistic community by helping normalize multilingualism.
- Engaging in shared learning and peer collaboration that is inclusive of multilingual learners.
- ______________________________
- ______________________________

(I invite you to continue the list by inviting student and teacher input)

Pause for a Moment

How can multilingual learners demonstrate their agency and take ownership of a multilingual future?

What additional roles and responsibilities may all students take on to advance equity and justice?

With whom and how might multilingual learners collaborate to ensure a prosperous future?

What Teachers Can Do to Sustain Multilingual Justice and Equity

Educators have a critical role in creating a caring, safe learning space for all students, including multilingual learners, in and out of their classrooms, in every possible nook of the school building. That includes instructional and non-instructional spaces, such as the library, the gym, the playground, the school yard, the hallway, the cafeteria, and all other parts of a building and the surrounding areas. April Baker-Bell (2020) argues for linguistic safe havens "where students' language practices [are] affirmed, valued, and sustained" (p. 4). Students must feel supported by trusted adults in their lives, so educators have a crucial role of advocacy to stand up against negative forces that might want to crush students' multilingual assets.

In addition to safe learning environments, educators must also provide language-rich curricular and enrichment activities along with varied, language-focused, collaborative learning opportunities that tap into students' full linguistic repertoires—every educator, every day, in every classroom! We need more teachers who are formally prepared, credentialed, and certified as bilingual and ELD educators, who often take on the role of "boundary spanners, border crossers, and advocates" (Scanlan & Johnson, 2021, p. 227). But the responsibility to sustain multilingual justice cannot rest only on credentialed and certified specialists' shoulders. Bilingual/multilingual educators bring their own lived personal, familial, and social experiences, complex perspectives, and unique professional stance to schools. They are well positioned to be teacher leaders, their insights must be valued and talents nurtured, both for their own advancements and for their advocacy roles in a predominantly English-speaking school and larger community. Their role in ensuring multilingual equity through their day-to-day work, interaction with members of the school and larger community is crucial. All educators need to commit to and learn to sustain multilingual justice in their instructional and assessment practices through on-going, targeted professional development.

Tapestry of Voices

Luis Valentino, author and executive coach, offers his definition of multilingual equity and justice and three recommendations to sustain it:

Multilingual justice is the right to maintain linguistic diversity without facing discrimination or pressure to conform to the monolingual norm. Multilingual justice recognizes multilingualism as a cognitive and cultural superpower that is rooted in our lived experiences, where language and culture share an existential context. When we devalue someone's language, we diminish their cultural identity and lived experiences. True multilingual justice challenges a historical perspective of linguistic diversity as a problem rather than an asset. Multilingual justice calls for new and transformative policies that acknowledge and celebrate language diversity as valuable resources.

To sustain multilingual equity and justice:

1. *Build deep equity literacy through continuous professional learning*
2. *Cultivate collective leadership and allyship*
3. *Align policies and practices with equity commitments*

Sustained Professional Learning

The Learning Forward (2026) Standards for Professional Learning emphasize that the most effective professional development occurs in sustained, collaborative communities where educators engage in ongoing inquiry, reflection, and application. These standards highlight the importance of equity-driven practices, rigorous content aligned with curriculum and instruction, and professional expertise that fosters continuous growth. Additionally, the standards identify the conditions necessary for success, including effective leadership, equitable resource distribution, and a culture of shared responsibility. Here I advocate for the target content of carefully designed professional learning opportunities to be directly connected to what you and your team uncovered through the shadowing experiences, multilingual equity walks, and the equity audits I introduced in earlier chapters. The frequently utilized one-and-done or sit-and-get formats may be labelled and checked off as professional development, but they must be replaced with carefully designed, sustained learning opportunities.

Notable Research

Sam Sims and his team conducted a comprehensive meta-analytic study and developed a new framework they call IMTP to determine what makes in-service professional development effective:

> *In summary, we propose that PD needs to pay careful attention to four things if it is to bring about sustained improvements in teaching. First, it needs to provide insight (I) about teaching and learning… Second, PD should motivate (M) teachers to make changes to their practice… Third, PD should provide techniques (T) for putting these insights to work… Fourth, PD must embed that change in practice (P)… When PD succeeds in addressing I, M, T, and P, it is more likely to be effective.*
>
> (Sims et al., 2023, pp. 217–218)

When one or more of the four crucial elements are missing, the consequences may include widening the knowing-doing gap, teachers reverting to established habits, or failing to understand the "why" of the practice, thus leading to misapplication of strategies.

In my field-based research and coaching experiences with Maria G. Dove, we found that not only must teacher collaboration be the foundation of planning and delivering instruction for multilingual learners, but so does professional learning (Honigsfeld & Dove, 2026). Collaborative professional learning is characterized by (a) clear purpose and co-constructed goals for shared professional learning, (b) on-going focused exploration of what works for multilingual learners, (c) open communication and a willingness to share successes and challenges, (d) evidence-based discussions to guide further collaborative learning efforts, and (e) celebration of growth that highlights teacher achievement and classroom success. Table 6.1 offers a summary of joint professional learning practices with a focus on both sustaining multilingual equity and justice as well as promoting professional communities. As

Table 6.1 Joint professional learning with a focus on multilingual equity and justice.

Joint professional learning practices	To sustain multilingual equity and justice
Collegial circles	Teachers meet on a regular basis to discuss common questions, share concerns, offer solutions to common challenges, and suggest appropriate instructional techniques.
Peer intervisitations	All teachers of multilingual learners visit one another's classes to observe the teaching-learning process and multilingual learner outcomes in the classroom.
Collaborative coaching and mentoring	Teachers support each other's practice through a framework of modelling effective instruction and providing ongoing, student-centered classroom assistance for one another.
Research and development	Teachers collaboratively study and review research related to multilingualism and multilingual learners and plan and implement lessons based on their studies.
Collaborative inquiry (Action research)	Teachers participate in an in-depth exploration of an overarching concept that deals with multilingualism and multilingual learners.
Lesson study	Teachers jointly plan a lesson in response to a preestablished study question or goal. Through repeated lesson observations and discussions, teachers revise the lesson as it is re-taught and observed in each new class.
Professional-learning communities (PLCs)	Teachers work in PLCs and create a structure for improving schools by establishing and enacting a collaborative school culture and a collective purpose for learning.
Collaborative-learning teams (CLTs)	Teachers work in CLTs and—through shared goals, regular meetings, and an organized approach—engage in professional learning focused on effective instruction.

Source: adapted from Honigsfeld and Dove (2026)

you read through the choices, reflect on which of them are already successfully implemented in your context, which of them could receive more attention, which of them might be a worthy new initiative.

Tapestry of Voices

Jon Nordmeyer, School Network Director of the Multilingual Learning Research Center (MLRC) at the University of Wisconsin-Madison, shares that the goal of the MLRC is to advance educational outcomes for multilingual learners through innovative and socially just research and research–practice partnerships.

> *MLRC has designed a global research-practice partnership serving 150 schools across 60 countries. This global network cultivates equity by centering multilingual learners and their families as educators learn about and implement evidence-informed classroom practices related to translanguaging, teacher collaboration and the intersection of multilingualism and neurodiversity. For example, teachers and school leaders learn about translanguaging, both as a student practice and a pedagogical approach. Building on this foundation, the MLRC language policy working group connects educators across contexts to interrogate language ideologies and restrictive language policies. The MLRC also leverages the power of action research to disrupt the historical power relationships between universities and schools. By democratizing access to educational research, and building practitioners' understanding of the research process, the MLRC empowers practitioners to become both critical consumers and authentic producers of knowledge. Over the course of a semester, teams are supported through in-person research symposia and online support. The resulting school-based action research projects shed light on problems of practice at the local level, and teams share their research findings across the global network. This type of disciplined inquiry helps teachers understand and address inequity at the systemic level; and it also builds the confidence and competence for teacher leaders to lead change at their schools.*

Pause for a Moment

How can traditional professional development approaches be challenged, and what steps can be taken to foster a more collaborative, inquiry-based culture among staff in your environment?
What have been the most impactful professional learning opportunities you have participated in? Why?

What Coaches and Instructional Leaders Can Do to Sustain Multilingual Justice and Equity

Many schools rely on coaches and administrators taking on instructional leadership roles to support instructional consistency and foster discussions about what students need to be successful. Co-construction of curriculum inclusive of multilingual learners and instructional consistency with pathways to multilingual success must be added to goals of coaching and instructional leadership.

Hayley Weddle and colleagues (2024) suggest that "promoting equity for [multilingual] students within schools extends beyond teachers' practices to encompass a range of mindsets, norms, and structures" (p. 253). Instructional leaders who include coaches, teacher leaders, department heads, and administrators play a crucial role in shaping a positive, unified, and growth-oriented school culture that honors multilingualism, shapes educators' shared beliefs and collective mindsets about what students can do, and shifts norms and structures in a more equitable direction. When members of an instructional leadership team choose a collaborative approach, they move away from traditional top-down decision-making and embrace collective responsibility, ensuring that the shifts and changes are more consistent with the overall vision. According to Peter DeWitt (2018), "collaborative leadership is about growth. It's about fostering the growth of different stakeholders; it's about fostering our own growth as leaders; and it's about going deeper in our learning and with our relationships" (pp. 16–17), thus collaboration also contributes to sustaining change.

When coaches, instructional leaders, and staff work together, each person understands how their individual purpose aligns with and complements the work of colleagues. Such interconnectedness fosters trust, strengthens professional relationships, and enhances the group's ability to respond to challenges with unity. When members of a school community feel supported by a shared purpose, they are more likely to stay engaged, contribute their expertise, and grow together. Such collective ownership of multilingual equity and justice must be prioritized whether the challenge is to establish a more collaborative school culture, make joint decisions about new curriculum adaptations, or engage in ongoing analysis of assessment data.

Notable Research

Lisa Auslander and Joanna Yip (2022) identified organizational and structural changes that are needed to create the conditions for impactful teaching for multilingual learners. They highlighted four levers of change designed to support the systemic implementation of culturally, historically, and linguistically responsive and sustaining pedagogies:

1 Developing integrated and sustainable team learning: to maximize collective teacher efficacy and harness educators' collaborative expertise.
2 Integrating social-emotional learning into school-wide structures for planning and instruction: to ensure multilingual learners' academic, affective and linguistic development.
3 Establishing culturally and linguistically responsive data practices to inform teaching and learning: to identify the patterns of strengths and areas of needs among multilingual learners.
4 Deepening leadership practice and organizational learning for school improvement: to ensure all members are working towards shared goals and purposes with consistency and alignment.

Tapestry of Voices

Joanna Yip, Consultant and Executive Coach, whose research was cited above further highlights the need for a joint effort and a collaborative approach to leadership for equity:

Fighting for linguistic justice should be a collective effort. It's not something only multilingual people do. Some of us are on the hook for more but everyone is on the hook for something. Communities that choose collective responsibility and shared accountability prepare students for the realities and promises of a multilingual and multicultural future. To do this, we need leaders to build cross-functional teams that distribute responsibility for linguistic justice and normalize the expectation that supporting multilingualism is everyone's job.

What School, District, and State Administrators Can Do to Sustain Multilingual Justice and Equity

Advancing equity and multilingual justice also requires administrative leadership practices at the school, district, and state levels to intentionally dismantle systemic barriers and to cultivate inclusive communities rooted in respect, shared accountability, and equitable opportunity (Capper et al., 2020). The complexity of the task is well captured by a seminal research study that connected social justice leadership and superintendents' roles. At the core of the challenges superintendents face is to successfully connect the "political realm of the school board, the social realm of the community, and the pedagogical realm of teaching and learning" (Devono & Price, 2012, p. 5). What may successfully span these realms include creating and maintaining a shared vision of inclusion, building trust in the community and partnering with families, and ensuring high expectations and excellence from all. In addition to these findings, an expanding body of research on social justice leadership may be applied to achieving and sustaining multilingual equity and justice. For it to happen, leadership teams must be committed to the following:

- Creating an inclusive, welcoming school learning community with a shared vision of respect and acceptance of everyone's cultural and linguistic heritage and background.
- Ensuring a faculty and staff with more inclusive community representation and recruiting and retaining multilingual faculty and staff.
- Building a professional learning community that continually engages in collaborative inquiry that uncovers students' strengths, talents, and assets not merely their needs or linguistic, academic, and cultural challenges.
- Offering ongoing coaching support so all educators can expand their knowledge and skills about working with multilingual learners (Calderón, 2025).
- Establishing "flexible teaming" that allows for both horizontal (on grade level) and vertical (across grade level) teacher teams, as well as cross-disciplinary teamwork to support multilingual learners' curricular, instructional, and extracurricular needs.
- Connecting the district and school to community resources.
- ____________________
- ____________________

(I invite you to continue the list by inviting input from leadership team members.)

Tapestry of Voices

Michael Rodríguez, Executive Director of Dual Language Education of New Mexico highlights four ways to cultivate and sustain equity for multilingual justice, emphasizing the role of leadership:

Unless equity is embedded in every decision and systemic fabric of the school/organization, the ability to recognize, respond, redress or sustain efforts will be superficial. Cultivating and sustaining equity means:

1 *A commitment (in a very public way) to multilingual justice by top leaders.*
2 *Actions, through policy, procedures, accountability at every level.*
3 *Engaging in the difficult conversations and providing ongoing training.*
4 *Ensuring that all stakeholders are crystal clear about the approach, beliefs, and behaviors that are expected by every member within the system.*

Ingrid Corpuz, Program Manager of Title III Multilingual Learner Program at the South Carolina Department of Education and Adjunct Professor at St. Joseph's University (Bilingual Studies, TESOL, and Educational Leadership Programs), considers the roles she holds more than a job. It is a calling to make an impact as a justice-minded leader and advocate for multilingual learners:

I ground my work in the belief that every student's language and identity are powerful assets deserving recognition, belonging, and meaningful access to opportunity. Through intentional collaboration, I strive to support learning experiences that equip and empower multilingual learners, while honoring students' full humanity and holding high expectations for all. My commitment is to students, their families, their teachers, and the leaders who walk beside them. This is more than a professional role. It is a calling shaped by my own journey and the communities I serve. It is a responsibility I carry with deep gratitude and purpose.

Pause for a Moment

What aspects of equity leadership do you find most critical for multilingual justice?

What do you most admire about leaders who are able to lead with equity in mind?

How Caregivers, Parents, Families, and Community Members Can Sustain Multilingual Justice and Equity

If the adage is true and it takes a village to raise a child, it is also for raising a child multilingually. Multilingual families and other multilingual members of the community must remain committed to their cultural and linguistic heritages and continue to foster home language use and biliteracy or multiliteracy development. Forming partnerships within the school community and actively participating in advisory boards, councils, or parent-teacher associations or organizations all ensure ongoing communication and active engagement. Multilingual caregivers *must be and must feel* empowered as valued and respected members of the community.

Language assistance or language access services, including interpreters and translated resources must be readily available to ensure all multilingual members of the community are fully informed. But rather than merely being passive recipients of information, or simply offering feedback on already established policies, they must be able to meaningfully contribute to the decisions about their children and communicate their aspirations for their future! This is especially critical when it comes to advocating against and actively rejecting any historically harmful discriminatory practices such as forced transportation and segregation of multilingual learners/English learners into schools far from the families' neighborhood; tracking multilingual students into lower-level or remedial course work, inequitable assessment practices that inaccurately measure and, as a result, exclude multilingual learners from a range of academic opportunities; lack of high quality culturally and linguistically responsive and sustaining instructional resources.

It's easier said than done! Here are some strategies to counteract linguicism and discrimination that families and community members encounter and to foster advocacy for multilingual equity and justice:

- Continuing to use and take great pride in heritage and home language(s).
- Discuss with children the importance of cultural and linguistic heritage.
- Initiate communication with teachers and administrators about family and community experiences with languages and the need to be fully included.
- Work with family and community liaisons who connect schools and families.
- Tap into community organizations to ensure students have rich opportunities to maintain their language and culture and find mentors and resources in multiple languages.
- Volunteer and bring their talents and expertise to the school community.
- Initiate after school and enrichment opportunities housed in the school building (if feasible).
- ______________________________
- ______________________________

(I invite you to continue the list by inviting family and community input.)

Spotlight on Multilingual Justice

Marguerite Lukes, Director of Research and Lara Evangelista, Executive Director share the evolution of Internationals Network for Public Schools as a powerful example of sustaining multilingual justice:

Back in 1985, a small group of teachers in New York City public schools jumped at the opportunity to design a small public high school tailored to meet the needs of recently arrived immigrant multilingual students. As seasoned educators of adolescent newcomers, they knew all too well the realities of comprehensive high schools for this population of students. They named their pilot newcomer school "International" because the students in it come from around the world. More than 40 years later, what began as a handful of innovative, child-centered, district-run secondary schools has grown into a national network of more than 30 high-performing public newcomer schools across the United States, serving over 10,000 students each year and leveraging peer learning across schools, districts, and states.

From its earliest days, the Internationals Network was founded on a simple but radical premise: multilingual learners thrive when schools are intentionally designed around their strengths, identities, and aspirations—not when they are expected to adapt to systems built without them in mind. Rather than separating language development from academic learning, Internationals schools integrate rigorous content, language growth, and social-emotional development through collaborative, project-based instruction. Students learn in heterogeneous classrooms where language is treated as an asset, peer interaction is central to learning, and performance-based assessments replace reliance on high-stakes testing alone.

This commitment to equity has never been episodic. It is sustained through structures, practices, and professional cultures that make multilingual justice part of everyday school life.

Sustaining Equity Through Coherent Systems

Equity at Internationals is not a standalone initiative; it is embedded across curriculum, assessment, staffing, and leadership. Instruction is designed around collaborative learning, allowing students to build academic language while engaging deeply with grade-level content. Teachers regularly co-plan interdisciplinary units that connect academic concepts to students' lived experiences, cultures, and communities. Data are used formatively—not to label students, but to refine instruction and identify opportunities for support.

Equally important is the Network's commitment to distributed leadership. Schools are organized around shared responsibility rather than hierarchical control. Teachers, instructional coaches, counselors, and administrators work together in professional learning communities to analyze student work, reflect on practice, and design improvements. This collective approach ensures that equity does not depend on individual champions; instead, it becomes a shared organizational responsibility that can endure staff turnover and shifting policy contexts.

A Whole-Child Approach to Newcomer Success

Internationals schools recognize that academic achievement cannot be separated from students' emotional well-being, sense of belonging, and identity development. Many newcomer youth arrive having experienced disrupted schooling, migration stress, or social isolation. In response, schools adopt a whole-child framework that integrates counseling, advisory systems, restorative practices, and culturally responsive pedagogy.

Internationals students are known well by adults who serve not only as teachers but also as advocates and mentors. Advisory periods create space for relationship-building, goal-setting, and reflection. Classroom practices emphasize voice, collaboration, and mutual respect, fostering environments where students feel safe taking linguistic and intellectual risks. This holistic approach strengthens engagement, persistence, and confidence—foundational conditions for long-term academic success.

Supporting Teachers as Professionals and Learners

A defining feature of the Network's sustainability is its investment in educators as both professionals and continuous learners. Internationals schools are intentionally designed as learning organizations. Teachers participate in job-embedded professional development through co-teaching, peer observation, instructional coaching, and network-wide communities of practice.

Rather than relying on isolated workshops, professional learning is embedded in the rhythm of the school day. This is made possible through a structure intentionally designed into Internationals schools: interdisciplinary teacher teams who share a cohort of students and have scheduled planning time to collaborate, learn from one another, and provide mutual support. Educators regularly analyze student work, experiment with instructional strategies, and receive ongoing feedback from colleagues. Many also take on leadership roles as mentor teachers, facilitators, or curriculum designers—creating clear pathways for professional growth while strengthening collective capacity across the school.

This collaborative professional culture not only improves instructional quality; it also supports retention. Teachers report feeling valued, intellectually engaged, and connected to a larger mission—conditions that help stabilize staffing in schools serving high-need populations.

Partnering With Families and Communities

Multilingual justice also depends on strong partnerships beyond school walls. Internationals schools work closely with families, recognizing them as essential partners in students' learning journeys. Communication is multilingual and culturally responsive, and schools actively create opportunities for families to participate in school life, from workshops and conferences to community celebrations.

Equally vital are partnerships with community-based organizations that provide health services, legal support, college advising, workforce development, and enrichment opportunities. These collaborations expand the ecosystem of care around students, addressing barriers that schools cannot solve alone. By integrating community resources into school programming, Internationals ensures that students receive coordinated support across academic, social, and practical domains.

Lessons for Sustaining Multilingual Justice

The Internationals Network offers an important lesson for policymakers and educators seeking to advance multilingual justice: sustainable equity is built through aligned systems, not isolated interventions. It requires intentional staffing models, collaborative professional cultures, whole-child supports, and authentic partnerships with families and communities.

Perhaps most importantly, it requires a long-term commitment to seeing multilingual learners not as temporary guests in the education system, but as central participants whose languages, experiences, and perspectives enrich school communities. Four decades after its founding, the Network demonstrates what becomes possible when schools are designed around this belief—and when justice is treated not as a destination, but as an ongoing practice.

Learn more about Internationals Network at www.internationalsnetwork.org

Pause for a Moment

Inspired by the Spotlight story, what specific structures, policies, or collaborative practices could be implemented in your context to move equity from an individual initiative to a sustainable, collective responsibility?

In what ways can multilingual learners' social-emotional well-being impact their sense of belonging and academic success, which, in turn, can foster equity and justice?

Moving Beyond Sustaining Multilingual Justice

My most sincere hope is that we achieve, cultivate and sustain multilingual justice for all students. How might we move beyond achieving the highest level of equity literacy? Keep the equity work going. In the field of education, when we think we are done, we are just getting started to go deeper and to expand our impact into wider spheres! Connect with me on social media or email me at mlequityandjustice@gmail.com with your accomplishments and success stories.

End-of-Chapter Reflections

As you finish exploring the final ability of equity literacy, reflect on the following:

- ★ Why do mission, vision, and value statements matter?
- ★ How do you see educators' roles in advancing multilingual justice and how does sustained professional learning impact teachers' own agency to make a difference?
- ★ How can multilingual learners and their families benefit from sustained multilingual justice?

Epilogue

Flying High

Dedicated to all of you flying high

Have you ever heard the roar of silence?
Have you ever listened to the shriek of indifference?
Have you ever seen hypocrisy dressed up in fancy garbs of love?
Have you ever been blinded by the thick fog of injustice?
Have you ever tried to swim in a stream made of solid rock?
Have you ever inhaled fire then swallowed it whole?
Have you ever been pushed, pushed aside, pushed down, pushed out,
pushed
and
pushed
and
pushed so hard that falling was never even an option …
… you had to fly instead?

DOI: 10.4324/9781003644071-7

IF you
HAVE,
just
FLY
HIGH
AND
and
SOAR
I WILL
SEE
you
UP
THERE

Appendix A

Delphi Study

In preparation for writing this book, I have taken an elaborate and creative approach to defining multilingual justice. Inspired by a variation of the Delphi approach (RAND, 2025), I created a modified protocol of this most intriguing qualitative research method. I assembled a panel of internationally recognized experts on multilingualism and invited them to participate in two rounds of surveys and either a focus group discussion or an individual interview as a final step to the process. As intended by the originators of the Delphi method, the goal is consensus building around a complex concept while considering multiple perspectives and nuanced differences in understanding. Although this volume is not written as a research monograph, it was important to me to add scholarly depth to this essential topic and treat it with the utmost reverence and care it deserves. The adapted version of the Delphi method helped me achieve this precision by surrounding myself with brilliant minds over the course of 4 months as we engaged in the following:

Phase 1: I invited over 50 internationally recognized experts of multilingual education. In the end, 34 agreed to participate in one or several phases of the study (see below for their names). A modified Delphi protocol was introduced, which included keeping members of the panel anonymous to each other until the final phase of the protocol.

Phase 2: Members of the panel responded to the first survey, the goal of which was to gather everyone's baseline definition of what multilingual justice vs. injustice is and how these two concepts manifest themselves in educational and larger societal contexts.

Phase 3: The purpose of the second survey was to bring divergent perspectives together and establish consensus around what multilingual justice/injustice is. I manually coded as well as used three different AI tools (Gemini, Claude, and ChatGPT) to analyze the data and generate possible definitions. After consolidating the 30+ responses to each prompt in Survey 1 to three choices for both, I invited the panelists to rank them to help determine the most comprehensive shared definition of multilingual justice/injustice. In addition, the second survey requested input into the types of abilities this book would unpack to achieve multilingual justice.

Phase 4: As an augmentation to the classic Delphi approach, the expert panelists were invited to participate in one of three optional focus group sessions and/or individual interviews to engage in further discussion about what multilingual justice and injustice are in the educational setting. These recorded conversations added additional depth to our shared exploration of what is multilingual justice and what counts as injustice, what matters in K-12 education and beyond and how we work collectively to achieve multilingual justice.

Members of the Delphi panel alphabetically listed:

Laura Ascenzi-Moreno
Tim Boals
Julie Esparza Brown
Stacy Brown
Ying Chu
Ayanna Cooper
Ester de Jong
Kathy Escamilla
Montserrat Garibay
Margo Gottlieb
Andrea Hellman
Tatyana Kleyn
Joanna Kolota
Joan Lachance
Christine Montecillo Leider
Ching-Ching Lin
Aradhana Mudambi
Diep Nguyen
Luciana de Oliveira
Michael Rodríguez
David Rogers
Shadia Salem
Cristina Sánchez-López
Ali Fuad Selvi
Robert Sharples
Deborah Short
Diane Staehr Fenner
Julie Sugarman
Luis Valentino
Ruslana Westerlund
Kevin Wong
Wayne Wright
Justin Zhang
Jeff Zwiers

Appendix B

Myths or Facts?

All of the statements in the "Myths or Facts?" section of Chapter 2 are myths or misconceptions. Resources to consult for a complete explanation of these myths and misconceptions can be found here:

Borges, R., & Lyddy, F. (2024). Language affects endorsement of misconceptions about bilingualism. *International Journal of Bilingual Education and Bilingualism, 27*(2), 230–239.

Costa, J. (2023). *Common misconceptions about teaching multilingual learners to read (and how they keep students from meeting their potential).* https://instructionpartners.org/2023/03/27/common-misconceptions-about-teaching-multilingual-learners-to-read

Kroll, J. F., & Dussias, P. E. (2017). The benefits of multilingualism to the personal and professional development of residents of the US. *Foreign Language Annals, 50*(2), 248–259.

National Academies of Sciences, Engineering, and Medicine. (2017). *Dual language learners and English learners with disabilities.* www.nap.edu/resource/24677/toolkit/pdf/6-DLs&ELs-with-Disabilities.pdf

References

Aguilar, E. (2021). *Coaching for equity: Conversations that change practice*. Jossey-Bass.

Alim, H. S., Reyes A., & Kroskrity, P. (Eds.). (2020). *Oxford handbook of language and race*. Oxford University Press.

American Community Survey. (2019). *1-year estimates-public use microdata sample*. Detailed home language. U.S. Department of Commerce, U.S. Census Bureau.

Ardell, L. (2025). *Disrupting the monolingual bias: A framework for teacher advocacy*. Corwin.

Auslander, L., & Yip, J. (2022). *School-wide systems for multilingual learner success: A roadmap for leaders*. Routledge.

Avineri, N., & Baquedano-López, P. (2024). *An introduction to language and social justice: What is, what has been, and what could be*. Routledge.

Baker-Bell, A. (2020). *Linguistic justice: Black language, literacy, identity, and pedagogy*. Routledge.

Banks, J. (2019). Approaches to multicultural curriculum reform. In J. A. Banks & C. A. McGee Banks (Eds.), *Multicultural education: Issues and perspectives* (10th edition, pp. 137–157). John Wiley.

Becker, A. L. (1991). Language and languaging. *Language & Communication*, *11*(1–2), 33–35.

Bennett, R. E. (2023). Toward a theory of socioculturally responsive assessment. *Educational Assessment*, *28*(2), 83–104.

Bernstein, K. A., Henderson, K. I., Chaparro, S., & Alvarez, A. (2024). Creating DLBE programs that center equity in the face of school choice policies. In M. G. Delavan, J. A. Freire, & K. Menken (Eds.), *The gentrification of dual language, bilingual and immersion education: Solution-oriented research and stakeholder resources for real integration* (pp. 271–284). Multilingual Matters.

Blankstein, A. M. (2013). *Failure is not an option: 6 principles that advance student achievement in highly effective schools*. Corwin.

Bolman, L. G., & Deal, T. E. (2021). *Reframing organizations: Artistry, choice, and leadership* (7th edition). Wiley.

Britton, J. (1983). Writing and the story of the world. In B. Kroll & E. Wells (Eds.), *Explorations in the development of writing, theory, research, and practice* (pp. 3–30). Wiley.

Bunch, G. C., & Walqui, A. (2025). Educating multilingual learners. In A. Walqui, G. C. Bunch, & Mueller, P. (Eds.), *Amplifying the curriculum:*

Designing quality learning opportunities for multilingual learners (2nd edition, pp. 3–27). Teachers College Press.

Burton, J. (2025). "I am THAT refugee!" Raising Critical Multilingual Language Awareness through spoken word poetry with refugee-background learners. *TESOL Journal, 59*, 2179–2205.

Calderón, M. E. (2025). *Coaching for multilingual excellence: Strategies for vocabulary, reading, and writing across disciplines*. Corwin.

Capper, C. A., Young, M. D., & Frattura, E. (2020). The equity audit as the core of leading. In G. Theoharis & M. Scanlan (Eds.), *Leadership for increasingly diverse schools* (pp. 259–272). Routledge.

Cervantes-Soon, C. G., Dorner, L., Palmer, D., Heiman, D., Schwerdtfeger, R., & Choi, J. (2017). Combating inequalities in two-way language immersion programs: Toward critical consciousness in bilingual education spaces. *Review of Research in Education, 41*, 403–427.

Cervantes-Soon, C., Gambrell, J., Kasun, G. S., Sun, W., Freire J. A., & Dorner, L. M. (2021). "Everybody wants a choice" in dual language education of El Nuevo Sur: Whiteness as the gloss for everybody in media discourses of multilingual education. *Journal of Language, Identity & Education, 20*(6), 394–410

Charity Hudley, A. H., & Flores, N. (2022). Social justice in applied linguistics: Not a conclusion, but a way forward. *Annual Review of Applied Linguistics, 42*, 144–154.

Cioè-Peña, M. (2017). The intersectional gap: How bilingual students in the United States are excluded from inclusion. *International Journal of Inclusive Education, 21*(9), 906–919.

Cohn-Vargas, B., & Zacarian, D. (2024). *Identity safe spaces at home and school: Partnering to overcome inequity*. Teachers College Press.

Crawford, J. (2008). *Advocating for English learners: Selected essays*. Multilingual Matters.

Crawford, E. R., Aguayo, D., & Valle, F. (2022). Culturally responsive leadership for Latinx immigrant students: Advocacy in a US–Mexico border alternative school. *Journal of School Leadership, 32*(6), 586–611. https://doi.org/10.1177/10526846221095746

Crenshaw, K. (1989). Demarginalizing the intersection of race and sex: A Black feminist critique of antidiscrimination doctrine, feminist theory, and antiracist politics. *University of Chicago Legal Forum, 1*, 139–167. https://chicagounbound.uchicago.edu/cgi/viewcontent.cgi?article=1052&context=uclf

Cummins, J. (2001). *Negotiating identities: Education for empowerment for a diverse society*. California Association for Bilingual Education.

de Jong, E. J., Yilmaz, T., & Marichal, N. (2019). A multilingualism-as-a-resource orientation in dual language education. *Theory Into Practice, 58*, 107–120.

de Oliveira, L. C., & Terrell, K. L. (2026). *Preparing antiracist ESOL professionals: Linguistic equity for multilingual learners*. Routledge.

Devono, F., & Price, T. (2012, July). How principals and teachers perceived their superintendents' leadership in developing and supporting effective learning environments as measured by the Superintendent Efficacy Questionnaire. *National Forum of Educational Administration & Supervision Journal, 25*(4), 1–14.

DeWitt, P. M. (2018). *School climate: Leading with collective efficacy*. Corwin.

Donohoo, J., & Katz, S. (2019). *Quality implementation: Leveraging collective efficacy to make "what works" actually work*. Corwin.

Dove, M. G., Honigsfeld, A., & McDermott Goldman, C. (2026). *Nine dimensions of scaffolding for multilingual learners*. Corwin.

Dugan, J. (2022, October 1). Radical dreaming for education now. *Educational Leadership*. www.ascd.org/el/articles/radical-dreaming-for-education-now

Eklöf, T., Callahan, R., & Vogel, S. (2025). Lau Plans and rural ML-EL education: Self-assessment as a tool to support educational equity. *AASA Journal of Scholarship and Practice, 22*(3), 28–39. www.aasa.org/docs/default-source/publications/journal-of-scholarship-and-practice/fall-2025/lau-plans-and-rural-ml-el-education—evidence-article-fall-2025-jsp.pdf?sfvrsn=a1b43a6_1

Epstein, J. L., et al. (2019). *School, family, and community partnerships: Your handbook for action* (4th edition). Corwin Press.

Ernst-Slavit, G., & Gottlieb, M. (2026). *Academic languaging: Engaging multilingual students in content area learning*. Corwin.

Esteban-Guitart, M., & Moll, L. C. (2014). Lived experience, funds of identity and education. *Culture & Psychology, 20*, 70–81.

Estrada, P., Wang, H., & Farkas, T. (2020). Elementary English learner classroom composition and academic achievement: The role of classroom-level segregation, number of English proficiency levels, and opportunity to learn. *American Educational Research Journal, 57*(4), 1791–1836.

Ethnologue. (2025). *How many languages are there in the world*? www.ethnologue.com/insights/how-many-languages

Etymonline. (2026). *Cultivate*. www.etymonline.com/word/cultivate

Flores, N. (2020). From academic language to language architecture: Challenging raciolinguistic ideologies in research and practice. *Theory Into Practice, 59*(1), 22–31.

Flores, N. (2024). *Becoming the system: A raciolinguistic genealogy of bilingual education in the post-civil rights era*. Oxford University Press.

Flores, N., & Lewis, M. C. (2022). "False positives, reentry programs, and long-term English learners": Undoing dichotomous frames in U.S. language education policy. *Equity & Excellence in Education, 55*(3), 257–269.

Flores, N., & Rosa, J. (2015). Undoing appropriateness: Raciolinguistic ideologies and language diversity in education. *Harvard Educational Review, 85*(2), 149–171.

Freire, J. A., Feinauer, E., Earl, M., & Willardson, K. (2024). Critical consciousness in dual language bilingual education: A literature review of students' outcomes. In J.A. Freire, C. Alfaro, & E. de Jong (Eds.), *The handbook of dual language bilingual education* (pp. 213–232). Routledge.

Freire, P. (1998). *Pedagogy of freedom: Ethics, democracy and civic courage*. Rowman & Littlefield.

Frey, N., Fisher, D., & Nelson, J. (2013). Todo tiene que ver con lo que se habla: It's all about the talk. *Kappan, 94*(6), 8–13.

García, O., Kleifgen, J. A., & Cervantes-Soon, C. (2025). *Educating emergent bilinguals: Policies, programs, and practices for multilingual learners* (3rd edition). Teachers College Press.

García, O., & Wei, L. (2014). *Translanguaging: Language, bilingualism and education*. Springer.

Garmston, R. J., & Wellman, B. M. (2016). *The adaptive school: A sourcebook for developing collaborative groups* (3rd edition). Bloomsbury.

Gebhard, M., & Accurso, K. (2023). Pursuing a multilingual equity agenda: SFL and teacher action research in hard times. In M. Gebhard & K. Accurso (Eds.), *In pursuit of a multilingual equity agenda: SFL teacher action research* (pp. 1–30). Routledge.

Gibson, M. (2024). Translanguaging as embodied civic practice: Centering language in civic educational practice and research. In A. T. Jaffe & C. Salinas (Eds.), *Teaching culturally and linguistically relevant social studies for emergent bilingual and multilingual youth* (pp. 19–33). Teachers College Press.

Gonzalez, N., Moll, L. C., & Amanti, C. (2005). *Funds of knowledge: Theorizing practices in households, communities, and classrooms*. Erlbaum.

Gorski, P. (n.d). *Equity literacy: Definition and abilities*. www.equityliteracy.org/equity-literacy-definition

Gorski, P., & Swalwell, K. (2023a). *Fix injustice, not kids, and other principles for transformative equity leadership*. ASCD.

Gorski, P., & Swalwell, K. (2023b). Moving from equity awareness to action. *Educational Leadership, 80*(8), 20–27.

Gottlieb, M. (2021). *Classroom assessment in multiple languages: A handbook for teachers*. Corwin.

Gottlieb, M. (2022). *Assessment in multiple languages: A handbook for school and district administrators*. Corwin.

Gottlieb, M. (2024). *Assessing multilingual learners: Bridges to empowerment*. (3rd edition). Corwin.

Gottlieb, M., & Honigsfeld, A. (2020). From assessment *of* learning to assessment *for* and *as* learning. In M. E. Calderón, M. G. Dove,

D. S. Fenner, M. Gottlieb, A. Honigsfeld, T. W. Singer, S. Slakk, I. Soto, & D. Zacarian. *Breaking down the wall: Essential shifts for English learners' success* (pp. 135–160). Corwin.

Gottlieb, M., & Honigsfeld, A. (2025). *Collaborative assessment for multilingual learners and their teachers: Pathways to partnerships*. Corwin.

Green, T. L. (2017). Community-based equity audits: A practical approach for educational leaders to support equitable community-school improvements. *Educational Administration Quarterly, 53*(1), 3–39.

Gruenert, S., & Whitaker, T. (2024). *School culture rewired: Toward a more positive and productive school for all* (2nd edition). ASCD.

Hargreaves, A. (2019) Teacher collaboration: 30 years of research on its nature, forms, limitations and effects. *Teachers and Teaching, 25*(5), 603–621.

Hattie, J. (2018). *Collective teacher efficacy (CTE) according to John Hattie*. https://visible-learning.org/2018/03/collective-teacher-efficacy-hattie/

Hellman, A. B. (2024). TEAMS USA: A *Teaching English and Academics to Multilingual Students Using Strengths-based Approaches—A professional development course for school teams*. Show Me Multiliteracy Project.

Hofer, B. (2025). The multicompetent mind – how does early multilingualism affect children's language development and cognition? *Intercultural Education, 36*(5), 548–563.

Honigsfeld, A., & Cohan, A. (2024). *Collaboration for multilingual learners with exceptionalities: We share the students*. Corwin.

Honigsfeld, A., & Dove, M. G. (2022). *Co-planning: Five essential practices to integrate curriculum and instruction for English learners*. Corwin.

Honigsfeld, A., & Dove, M. G. (2026). *A leader's guide to collaboration and co-teaching for multilingual learners* (2nd edition). Corwin.

Honigsfeld, A., Dove, M. G., Cohan, A., & McDermott Goldman, C. (2022). *From equity insights to action: Critical strategies for teaching multilingual learners*. Corwin.

Howard, E. R., Lindholm-Leary, K. J., Rogers, D., Olague, N., Medina, J., Kennedy, B., Sugarman, J., & Christian, D. (2018). *Guiding principles for dual language education* (3rd edition). Center for Applied Linguistics.

Huang-Nissen, S. (1999). *Dialogue groups: A practical guide to facilitate diversity conversation*. Medicine Bear Pub.

Karam, F. J., & Kibler, A. K. (2025). Introduction: A vision for critical dialogic education within the context of TESOL teacher education. In F. J. Karam & A. K. Kibler (Eds.), *Critical dialogic TESOL teacher education: Preparing future advocates and supporters of multilingual learners* (pp. xi–xvi). Bloomsbury.

Kibler, A. (2023, May 8). *Why ecologies matter: Critical and dialogic perspectives on instruction, assessment, and policies impacting multilingual youth*

[Keynote presentation]. Improving Instruction, Assessment, and Policies for Secondary English Learners Across the Content Areas, Inaugural Conference, Washington, D.C., United States.

Kibler, A., Valdés, G., & Walqui, A. (Eds.). (2021). *Reconceptualizing the role of critical dialogue in American classrooms: Promoting equity through dialogic education*. Routledge.

Kieffer, M. J., & Weaver, A. W. (2024). Classroom concentration of English learners and their reading growth. *Educational Researcher, 53*(1), 54–58.

Kohl, K., & Ouyang, W. (2020). Introducing creative multilingualism. In K. Kohl, R. Dudrah, A. Gosler, S. Graham, M. Maiden, W. Ouyang, & M. Reynolds (Eds.), *Creative multilingualism: A manifesto* (pp. 1–25). Open Book Publishers.

Kroll, J., F., & Dussias, P. E. (2017). The benefits of multilingualism to the personal and professional development of residents of the US. *Foreign Language Annals, 50*(2), 248–259.

Kruse, S. D., Rodela, K. C., & Huggins, K. S. (2018). A regional network of superintendents confronting equity: Public and private messy messages. *Journal of School Leadership, 28*(1), 82–109. https://doi.org/10.1177/105268461802800104

Lachance, J., & Honigsfeld, A. (2023). *Collaboration and co-teaching for dual language learners: Transforming programs for multilingualism and equity*. Corwin.

Learning Forward. (2026). *Standards for professional learning*. https://standards.learningforward.org/standards-for-professional-learning

Lin, C.-C., & Uysal, H. (2025). *Centering multilingual learners in school curriculum through community asset mapping: A practical guide for teachers*. Myers Education Press.

List, A., & Dykeman, C. (2021). Disproportionalities in gifted and talented education enrollment rates: An analysis of the U.S. civil rights data collection series. *Preventing School Failure, 65*(2), 108–113. https://doi.org/10.1080/1045988X.2020.1837061

Liu, L. H., & Rao, R., with Silverman, C. A. (Eds.). (2024). *Global language justice*. Columbia University Press.

Maldonado Rodríguez, L. A., & Krause, G. (2020). Flowing with the translanguaging corriente: Juntos engaging with and making sense of mathematics. *Teaching for Excellence and Equity in Mathematics, 11*(2), 17–25.

Martínez-Álvarez, P. (2022). *Teacher education for inclusive bilingual contexts: Collective reflection to support emergent bilinguals with and without disabilities*. Routledge.

Menken, K., Espinet, I., & Avni, S. (2023). "There was nothing here": School leaders using Dual Language Bilingual Education programs as a formula to re-engineer student populations for school turnaround. *Educational Policy, 38*(2), 448–478.

MiSTEM Network. (n.d.). *3-P learning and YPAR. 3-P Learning and YPAR.* www.michigan.gov/-/media/Project/Websites/leo/Folder10/20-GVSU-0117-3P-Learning-YPAR-003-PP1.pdf

Niño, J. M., & Perez-Diaz, M. B. (2021). Social justice leaders serving students of color in Southwest Texas rural schools. *Journal of Research in Rural Education, 37*(7), 80–93.

NYSED. (n.d.) *Multilingual Learner/English Language Learner (MLL/ELL) Shadowing Protocol.* www.nysed.gov/sites/default/files/programs/bilingual-ed/mll-shadowing-protocol-appendix-a-final-a_0.pdf

Odabaş, M., & Aragão, C. (2022). *School district mission statements highlight a partisan divide over diversity, equity and inclusion in K–12 education.* www.pewresearch.org/social-trends/2023/04/04/school-district-mission-statements-highlight-a-partisan-divide-over-diversity-equity-and-inclusion-in-k-12-education

Office of the Attorney General. (2025). *Memorandum for All Federal Agencies.* www.justice.gov/ag/media/1407776/dl?inline=&utm_medium=email&utm_source=govdelivery

Ottow, S. B. (2023). *The language lens for content classrooms: A guidebook for teachers, coaches, and leaders* (2nd edition). Confianza LLC.

Pacheco, M. B., Daniel, S. M., Pray, L. C., & Jiménez, R. T. (2019). Translingual practice, strategic participation, and meaning-making. *Journal of Literacy Research, 51*(1), 75–99.

Palmer, D. L., Almager, I. L., Valle, F., Gabro, C., & deLeon, V. (2019a). Using equity audits to create a support system for marginalized students. *School Leadership Review, 14*(2). https://scholarworks.sfasu.edu/slr/vol14/iss2/9

Palmer, D. K., Cervantes-Soon, C., Dorner, L., & Heiman, D. (2019b). Bilingualism, biliteracy, biculturalism, and critical consciousness for all: Proposing a fourth fundamental goal for two-way dual language education, *Theory into Practice, 58*(2), 121–133.

Palmer, D., Meinzen, L., Milán, M., & Valladares, M. R. (2025). Caminos hacia el biliteracy: Developing critical consciousness through Youth Participatory Action Research. *MinneTESOL Journal, 41*(2). https://minnetesoljournal.org/wp-content/uploads/2025/12/Palmer-et-al._Caminos-hacia-el-biliteracy-Developing-critical-consciousness-through-youth-participatory-action-research.pdf

Parra, M. O., & Proctor, P. (2022). The translanguaging pedagogies continuum. *Journal of Education, 203*(4), 917–924.

Piller, I. (2016). *Linguistic diversity and social justice*. Oxford University Press.

Piller, I. (2021). Language and social justice. In J. Stanlaw (Ed.), *The International Encyclopedia of Linguistic Anthropology* (pp. 1–7). Wiley.

Pinar, W. F. (2004). *What is curriculum theory?* Erlbaum.

Pinar, W. F. (2023). *A praxis of presence in curriculum theory: Advancing* currere *against cultural crises in education*. Routledge.

Poarch, G. J., & Krott, A. (2019). A bilingual advantage? An appeal for a change in perspective and recommendations for future research. *Behavioral Sciences*, 9(9), 95. https://doi.org/10.3390/bs9090095

RAND. (2025). *Delphi method*. www.rand.org/topics/delphi-method.html

Roda, A., & Menken, K. (2024). The conflation of dual language bilingual education with gifted programs in New York City Schools. *Educational Policy, 39*(3), 531–571.

Ross, L. J. (2025). *Calling in: How to start making change with those you'd rather cancel*. Simon and Schuster.

Ruíz, R. (1984). Orientations in language planning. *NABE Journal*, *8*(2), 15–34. https://doi.org/10.1080/08855072.1984.10668464

Safir, S., & Dugan, J. (2021). *Street data: A next-generation model for equity, pedagogy, and school transformation*. Corwin.

Samie, A. (2025). *Intersectionality*. www.britannica.com/topic/intersectionality

Scanlan, M., & Johnson, L. (2021). Inclusive leadership on the social frontiers: Family and community engagement. In G. Theoharis & M. Scanlan (Eds.), *Leadership for increasingly diverse schools* (2nd edition, pp. 227–258). Routledge.

Sims, S., Fletcher-Wood, H., O'Mara-Eves, A., Cottingham, S., Stansfield, C., Goodrich, J., Van Herwegen, J., & Anders, J. (2023). Effective teacher professional development: New theory and a meta-analytic test. *Review of Educational Research*, *95*(2), 213–254.

Singleton, G. (2021). *Courageous conversations about race: A field guide for achieving equity in schools and beyond* (3rd edition). Corwin.

Soto, I. (2021). *Shadowing multilingual learners* (2nd edition). Corwin.

Sousa, D. (2022). *How the brain learns* (6th edition). Corwin.

Staehr-Fenner, D. (n.d.). *Common core for English language learners: Equity audit table*. www.colorincolorado.org/sites/default/files/blog/equity-audit-table.pdf

Swain, M. (2006). Languaging, agency and collaboration in advanced language proficiency. In H. Byrnes (Ed.), *Advanced language learning: The contribution of Halliday and Vygotsky* (pp. 95–108). Continuum.

TED Radio Hour. (2021). *Loretta J. Ross: What if we called people in, rather than calling them out?* www.npr.org/transcripts/1061209084

Tracy-Bronson, C. P. (2020). District-level inclusive special education leaders demonstrate social justice strategies. *Journal of Special Education Leadership, 33*(2), 59–77.

US Department of Education. (2017). *English learner toolkit for State and Local Education Agencies (SEAs and LEAs)*. https://ncela.ed.gov/educator-support/toolkits/english-learner-toolkit

van Nieuwerburgh, C., & Biswas-Diener, R. (2025). *Radical listening: The art of true connection*. Penguin Random House.

Vygotsky, L. S. (1978). *Mind in society: The development of higher psychological processes*. Harvard University Press.

Walqui, A., & van Lier, L. (2010). *Scaffolding the academic success of adolescent English language learners: A pedagogy of promise*. WestEd.

Weddle, H., Hopkins, M., Lowenhaupt, R., & Kangas, S. E. N. (2024). Shared responsibility for multilingual learners across levels of the education system. *Educational Researcher, 53*(4), 252–261.

Weil, Z. (2023). Do you ask the right questions? www.psychologytoday.com/us/blog/becoming-a-solutionary/202303/do-you-ask-the-right-questions

Wessel-Powell, C., Panos, A., & R. Weir, R. (2021). A year of equity: Community actions and invitations. *Literacy, 55*(1), 62–76.

Wheatley, M. J. (2009). *Turning to one another: Simple conversations to restore hope to the future*. Berrett-Koehler.

WIDA. (2020). WIDA English language development standards framework, 2020 edition: Kindergarten–Grade 12. https://wida.wisc.edu/sites/default/files/resource/WIDA-ELDStandards-Framework-2020.pdf

Wiggins, G. P., & McTighe, J. (2005). *Understanding by design* (2nd expanded edition). ASCD.

Xu, N., & Valdez, V. E. (2023). Introducing translanguaging as pedagogy: Unpacking preservice ESL teachers' language ideologies and practices. In A. Esmail, A. Pitre, A. Duhon-Ross McCallum, J. Blakely, & H. P. Baptiste (Eds.), *Literacy, vocabulary, and acculturation: A critical education triangle for English language learners* (pp. 93–100). Rowman & Littlefield.

Yazan, B. (2025). Series foreword. In F. J. Karam & A. K. Kibler (Eds.), *Critical dialogic TESOL teacher education: Preparing future advocates and supporters of multilingual learners* (pp. xi–xvi). Bloomsbury.

York-Barr, J., Sommers, W. A., Ghere, G. S., & Montie, J. (2016). *Reflective practice for renewing schools: An action guide for educators* (3rd edition). Corwin.

Zwiers, J. (2024). *Overhauling learning for multilingual students: An approach for achieving pedagogical justice*. Corwin.

Zwiers, J., & Crawford, M. (2024). *Academic conversations: Classroom talk that fosters critical thinking and content understandings*. Routledge.

Żywiczyński, P. (2018). *Language origins: From mythology to science*. Peter Lang.

For Product Safety Concerns and Information please contact our EU
representative GPSR@taylorandfrancis.com
Taylor & Francis Verlag GmbH, Kaufingerstraße 24, 80331 München, Germany

www.ingramcontent.com/pod-product-compliance
Lightning Source LLC
LaVergne TN
LVHW060532111026
849885LV00036B/375
9781041081678